Biography of Sir Arnold Lunn

Biography of
Sir Arnold Lunn

1888-1974

Elisabeth Hussey

Editor: Bruce Battrick

Copyright © 2014 Elisabeth Hussey
All rights reserved.

ISBN: 1505685893
ISBN 13: 9781505685893

"Publication jointly sponsored by: The Hotel Eiger, Murren & B. Battrick"
Library of Congress Control Number: 2014922686
CreateSpace Independent Publishing Platform
North Charleston, South Carolina

Table of Contents

Foreword - Remembering My Grandfather vii

Chapter 1	1887-1903 Early Influences	1
Chapter 2	1902-8 Harrow and Balliol	11
Chapter 3	1909-13 Climbing and Marriage to Mabel	21
Chapter 4	1914-18 World War I & After	35
Chapter 5	1919-24 The Golden Years	49
Chapter 6	1925-28 Hannes Schneider, Arlberg-Kandahar & Inferno	65
Chapter 7	1929-35 Catholicism - and Downhill - Accepted	75
Chapter 8	1936-39 Against Totalitarianism!	93
Chapter 9	1939-45 World War II	107
Chapter 10	1945-49 Back to Racing and Politics	119
Chapter 11	1950-56 Very Active in His 60s	133
Chapter 12	1957-61 Enjoying Good Arguments	147
Chapter 13	1961-63 Fighting Shamateurism and Marriage to Phyllis	163
Chapter 14	1964-69 Ski Racing Organization and 80th Birthday ...	179
Chapter 15	1970-74 "When you are over 80 you should only ski for pleasure"	195

Sir Arnold on the Eigerjoch in 1924

Foreword

Remembering My Grandfather
by Bernard Lunn

WHEN I WAS born in 1954, Arnold Lunn was already 66 years old, and by the time I was old enough to have a conversation with him he was in mid-70s. He insisted on seeing his grandchildren one at a time. That was a wise move. He could avoid being witness to my brother and I bashing each other and bragging about our skiing exploits. Instead, he could get our individual attention.

When in Switzerland, I would have dinner with him at the Jungfrau Hotel in Murren, as that was next door to the Jungfrau Lodge where he stayed in those days. He loved to have a debate, which required that I take the opposite side of the argument. As he loved debating the existence of God, he was happy to find that I was rebelling against the Catholicism of my boarding school in England. He delighted in crushing my feeble attempts at debate. He was certainly not giving me any handicap points for my age, which made me feel grown-up and respected.

Of course, now I get to rehash some of those debates in my mind without him having the ability to counter my arguments. Did anybody say that life is fair?

He was best when he was demolishing the arguments of the supposed rationalists, the materialists who had what was to him a rather boring "What you see is what you get" view of the World. He knew from direct experience during his time in the mountains that sometimes the boring old physical world opens up to reveal something that is eternal. So he rejected materialism. He thought that materialism was boring. He also thought it was scientifically and factually wrong. He delighted in showing me the flaws in the arguments of the evolutionary theory. I accepted his basic argument that evolution is a theory and not scientifically provable. To me it was too big a leap to go from that to accepting the alternative theory that the World was created by God in seven days.

His rather dry, intellectual religious views were one part of his world. The other part of his world was the mystical experience that he occasionally got in the mountains. My favorite quote - I think it is from his book "Mountains of Youth" - is:

"Only those who have climbed through the night can truly understand the benediction of the dawn".

He was using the word "benediction" as a literary analogy to describe how wonderfully warming and cheering and gorgeous the rising Sun was in the mountains after climbing all night in the dark. But he must have also had a religious feeling that informed his choice of words. In the following prayer, which he wrote himself and which I read at my father's funeral, he made this connection explicitly:

"Let me give thanks, dear Lord, in the frailty of age, for the beloved mountains of my youth, for the challenge of rock and for the joy of skiing, for the friends with whom I climbed and skied, and above all, dear Lord, for those moments of revelation when the temporal beauty of the mountains reinforces my faith in the Eternal Beauty which is not subject to decay."

Elisabeth Hussey's wonderful Biography describes his absent mindedness very well. It was fun to read her book and notice similar traits in myself and members of my family. My son, Jake, loves the story of him putting on two ties because he forgot he had already put on the first. As a kind stranger said to me when I left a coffee shop without my laptop bag: "You must have been thinking great thoughts." Those of us in the absent-minded club like having that as an excuse!

My grandfather would also occasionally forget somebody's name. Again, I can relate to that problem, and the story goes that a friend would often greet my grandfather on the streets of Murren in the European way, with a kiss on the cheek. This was remarkable enough to an Englishman born in the Victorian era, but although he liked the fellow and could remember many interesting conversations with him, he could not remember his name. His wife Phyllis tried to help him through word associations, getting Arnold to remember the name in association with his kissing habit. This did not work well. The next time they met again on the street, my grandfather greeted him warmly with:

"Ah, Dr. Kissinger, how nice to see you again!"

1

1887-1903 Early Influences

It may seem strange that the son of a British Methodist missionary, born in India, revolutionised the rules for ski racing and wrote books that converted many to Catholicism, but Arnold Lunn was a man of many contrasts and his own life was full of change. Not a natural sportsman, he grew to love the mountains and altered the emphasis of international ski racing from long-distance cross-country and jumping to steep downhill and slalom. Swift in repartee he would accept another's argument if new evidence showed it to be true. So when he found himself convinced by argument that Catholicism was the only true religion, he wrote books to convert others.

He also had the virtues that went with his deficiencies. Tremendously absentminded himself (he often wore two ties because he had forgotten that he had put on the first), he accepted as perfectly reasonable that other people forgot things. Few men are sympathetic, as he was, to their own faults when committed by others.

His father, Henry Lunn, was born in 1859, the son of a grocer who was also a Wesleyan Methodist preacher in the Lincolnshire village of West Ashby. Henry was open-minded enough to attend the Anglican services in the nearby village and was always interested in bringing people of different religions together. He had learnt to trade when still a boy. Needing to recoup some funds after succumbing to a card trick on a train journey, he discovered that he could make money by breeding bantams and mice of many colours (white, fawn, black, grey or piebald). He sold them by advertising in the columns of Exchange and Mart.

Later, he foresaw a successful future for the sport then called "sphairistike" and began selling equipment for it. He was right, for sphairistike developed into lawn tennis. In 1879, Henry sent out a circular advertising his sporting equipment. He paid the eminent Mr Harry Jones, Secretary of the All England Lawn Tennis and Croquet Club, twenty guineas to write an article for the circular. He charged 35 shillings for four rackets, some balls, posts and nets.

In the same year he patented a scoring dial to be fixed to a tennis racquet. The Prince of Wales and his brother both bought dials and other tennis equipment. So Henry promptly announced that his business was under royal patronage and added footballs and cricket bats to his stock. Arnold Lunn said of his father that he had had no taste or talent for games, but he had a flair for what was likely to succeed.

He prospered at a time when sports firms such as Gamages and Slazengers were just beginning and he might have followed their success. But he had a dream, which changed all his plans. In the dream he was walking with a friend past a large house, with a tennis court on which young men and women were playing. He turned to his friend and said: "This is my place. Those are my children. I have had great success, but there is not a spark of religion in the place." Henry was so impressed by the dream that he gave up trading and prepared to be a missionary.

He was not yet 21 and with the £1,000 earned from selling his business, he paid his way through Trinity College, Dublin, from 1883 to 1887, taking degrees in medicine and divinity. He was as good a student as he had been a salesman and was awarded the Oratory Medal of the Theological Society and the President's Medal for a prize essay.

Towards the end of his university days, he met Ethel, eldest daughter of Canon Moore, Rector of Midleton, County Cork, and Headmaster of Midleton College. Henry and Ethel were married on 12 July 1887. His marriage reinforced his ecumenical feelings. Three months later, qualified as a Doctor of Medicine, Henry left with Ethel to be a missionary in India. So it was in Madras on 18 April 1888 that Arnold Lunn was born. However, the family only stayed in India for a few months. Henry's health suffered in the climate, both he and the baby became ill. He had to abandon his vocation as a missionary and returned to England in November 1888.

He remained deeply involved in Christian reunion and founded a magazine called "The Review of the Churches". He planned a meeting of divines representing Anglicans, Presbyterians, Methodists and Baptists to discuss reunion. The first meeting was originally to take place in Vossvangen in Norway, where the divines would spend the days in winter sports and the evenings in conference. Two ships on which they were booked to travel to Norway were sunk. There had been some newspaper coverage of the proposed reunion, and when the second ship sank one newspaper carried a headline about Henry Lunn, saying "Before Jonah got on board."

Henry decided not to go to Norway and instead, in January 1892, he took 26 Reunionists to Grindelwald in Switzerland, a country he had never visited himself. The conference was a success ecumenically and financially, so he arranged a follow-up, also in Grindelwald, in the summer.

To this he invited the entire Anglican bench of bishops and the leading Free Churchmen as his guests. Other participants were charged £10 10s for the return fare from London and two weeks full board in the best hotels. The Baer Hotel, Grindelwald, charged 3.50 Swiss Francs per day when £1 bought 25 CHF. Again, the conference was a great success. Every denomination except the Roman Catholics sent representatives. Henry Lunn also found he had made £500 profit on the travel and accommodation costs. As a result, he founded Lunn's Tours, at first operating only in summer.

In the early years, the Lunn family spent much of their time in Switzerland and Arnold's first clear memory was of Grindelwald in flames in the summer of 1892 – when he was four and his brother Hugh, three. Much later he wrote:

"The Baer Hotel was the first to catch fire and our little chalet just below the Baer began to burn a few minutes later. My brother and I were enjoying a siesta when our German nurse rushed into the room and threw open the windows. She was in love with the cook at the Hotel and, such is the dramatic power of love, was firmly persuaded that he was sticking faithfully to the spit, continuing to roast beef while he himself was being transformed into roast man. In fact, he was quietly watching the flames from the village street, while our nurse called on the population to save him. We met him next day, in the best of health, the first big disillusion of my life."

An aunt tried to prevent Arnold seeing the fire by putting a handkerchief over his eyes, but she need not have worried. At four he was enthusiastic at the possibility of seeing someone roast to death. Afterwards he remembered with pleasure seeing the apples on the trees baked by the flames. What did scare him, though, was the indifference of the mountains to this tragedy. He was later to write: "The Eiger, insolently preening its snows in the blood-red haze of the catastrophe, really gripped me with fear. The mountains bind us by their very superiority to suffering. The unrelenting callousness that hurls the boulders down the gully in which we are pinned appeals to our primitive imaginations."

This attitude towards the mountains was to stay with him throughout his life. He loved them but never underestimated their power and indifference to man. At age six the first book that he read to himself was Whymper's "Scrambles Amongst the Alps", and it had a great effect on his imagination.

This epic tale of Whymper's dual with the Italians, the simultaneous assault on the mountains and Whymper's arrival on the summit just as the Italians reached the Pic Tyndale impressed him. He was also fascinated by Whymper's engravings, particularly that of a stone avalanche on the Matterhorn. He read and reread Martin Conway's "The Alps from End to End" and it had a potent influence on his own mountaineering ambitions.

As a small boy he had no desire to be a soldier or an engine driver. His interest in life began and ended with mountaineering. He and his younger brothers, Hugh and Brian, did not play at Red Indians, but at mountain guides. At the Grindelwald chalet they got hold of about twenty feet of clothes line and an ancient pickaxe, which belonged to the landlord. They practised climbing on a steepish slope of earth, grass and rocks, which they called Hill Difficulty. Solemnly they roped up and Arnold led. One day, while laboriously ascending, they were rudely interrupted by a little girl who ran easily up what they had treated as a perilous incline, disdainfully dodging the steps they had cut so carefully. The boys were understandably indignant.

When, in 1895, his nurse said he was to be taken up a mountain, he thought he knew exactly what to expect. "When the great day arrived I looked anxiously for the guide, complete with axe and rope, but there was no guide and the great adventure began in the railway station where the nurse took tickets for the Scheidegg. I followed her up the bridle path from the Scheidegg to the Lauberhorn with a sinking heart. When I reached the summit, I looked down the precipices on the other side. 'Do we go down there?' I asked hopefully. 'No' said my nurse."

Writing was another compulsion from an early age. He started a diary in January 1897, which still survives. Pencilled entries in a childish hand tell of highlights in his days. On Monday 4 January he wrote: "We had lessons as usual then we went out for a walk, then we came home for dinner and then went out in the gardin (sic) wher we met Tindel a freand of ours ….he told us his master's father had a calf on his farm which had 4 heads and 8 legs and it lived only 3 days."

A happier entry came on 1 March that year: "For the first time we saw our little sister. She was the nicest little girl in the World. She had nice black hair, though the poem says: Once London town there came a little baby with her hair of golden brown this pretty little lady. Mother was beaming with joy." Entries then became rather sparse and stopped after June.

But his interest in climbing remained and the desire to write was already developed. He started another booklet which survives, entitled "Climbs in Switzerland 1896". The first climb was the Brevent in August 1898 when Arnold was ten. It gives the height of the mountain, the height at the start of the climb, the height climbed and that he climbed with his father and brother Hugh. The book continues until 1904. On 2 September that year he took his mother and brother Brian with him up the Faulhorn in five hours. His only regret was that the mist rising from the valley gathered and they had no view.

Later he felt that this early enthusiasm had taught him useful lessons for his life in the mountains. "Perhaps we learnt more about rock climbing from casual scrambles on the minor rock summits than we should have learnt on bigger expeditions between guides. At least we learnt to walk. When my brother was seven and I was nine, we climbed in the same day the Faulhorn, Rothhorn and Simelihorn, seven thousand feet of climbing. Four years later we walked over the Greater Scheidegg to Meiringen before lunch and returned the same way in the afternoon to Grindelwald: thirty miles and some eight thousand feet of climbing in the day".

Those early years built up his love of the mountains. When he wrote later about visits to Switzerland in school holidays, he put it clearly: "Could any contrast be more intense than the sunlit joy of that first morning in Bern when the 'authentic air of Paradise' seemed to linger round the terrace, and the leaden despair of the return to Charing Cross in a fog?"

To those who complained that the Alps were overcrowded, he wrote much later: "To the superficial observer, the Tschuggen may seem an unattractive scree and slate peak, yet the actual top is a delightful yielding carpet of springy Alpine turf touched with the blue of late gentians. Who will, may spend untroubled hours here watching the clouds drifting across Jungfrau, and in the north the dark turquoise waters of Thun gleaming between the intervening hills. Solitary, remote and secluded, they will scarce remember the proximity of the hidden hotel and its heterogenous mob."

Henry Lunn's tours proved popular in Adelboden, Murren, Chateau d'Oex and Montana. He booked whole hotels for the exclusive use of his clients and insisted on strict rules – no drinking after 11pm and no dancing the bunny-hug, a lively dance of the time.

The English had acquired a taste for winter sports ever since September 1864, when Johannes Badrutt of St Moritz bet four of the guests in his

Kulm Hotel that they would find as much Sun there in winter as in summer. Badrutt won his bet and the English kept coming to avoid their own foggy winters and enjoy instead skating and toboganning in clear sunshine.

So, in 1898, the ten-year-old Arnold met another challenge, this time in Chamonix. Skiing was not nearly so popular then as other winter sports. Henry Lunn's clients all enjoyed skating and tobogganing, but it was he who introduced them to skiing. The local doctor, Dr Payot, had brought the first pair of skis to the Chamonix valley only a year before, and neither skis nor ski instructors were generally available. Henry Lunn brought both from Switzerland and one pair of skis was short, intended for Arnold.

In "Skiing", published in 1913, Arnold Lunn described his first skiing lessons. "A few of us, a very few, armed ourselves with ski and repaired to a neighbouring slope. A little group of men with toboggans halted on a path nearby and watched with curiosity. Our instructor, a guide, led off. He slid down the slope leaning heavily on a vast pole, and when he got to the bottom without falling we cheered. He gave us a word of advice: "Lean on your pole and if you wish to turn to the right you come round gradually by putting your stick on the right, and dragging yourself round on it."

The Scandinavians, who had always had to use skis to move about in winter, had perfected the telemark turn, with bindings loose at the heel. This did not give enough control on steep Alpine slopes so at this time the Austrian, Mathias Zdarsky, credited by many - Arnold Lunn among them - with being the father of alpine skiing, was teaching the stem on short skis in his Lilienfeld school. The tips of the skis were pressed together to form a wedge, so that the skier could control his speed and turn by weighting the lower ski. They used a single heavy pole. Zdarsky also ran competitions called slaloms to see how well skiers turned round poles, but they were judged on style not speed.

Vivian Caulfeild wrote a book called "How to Ski" in 1911, which described both telemark and stem-christie turns. He and Lunn constantly discussed and tried out different ski techniques. As late as the 1940's Caulfeild was still recommending the telemark turn, perfected by the Scandinavians with the heel of the front foot lifted and the toe steering it round.

Few visitors bothered to ski in Chamonix in 1898 and even the ten-year-old Arnold thought it a poor sport. You fell about so. Tobogganing was much simpler and more exciting. But winters followed in the Alps and gradually he began to enjoy skiing - as much he said for the view and the joy of new country as for the run home.

In 1900 he made his first expedition on ski, the ascent of the Scheidegg from Grindelwald, but it was not until his father brought the first winter sports parties to Adelboden in the winter of 1902-3 and Arnold went with them, that he really fell in love with skiing. W.R. Rickmers visited Adelboden the following winter and it was not until he appeared that skiing became generally popular. Rickmers, who had a Scottish wife, had learnt from Mathias Zdarsky, the Austrian pioneer at Lilienfeld.

When Vivian Caulfeild wrote "How to Ski" the doctrine of two sticks was proclaimed. Lunn always maintained that the quickest way down was straight without braking. The next quickest was straight, using the sticks to brake. Turning came later. Canon Savage, Percival Farrar and a few others were almost the only visitors who ever attempted even the smallest tours on ski.

As a boy, Arnold Lunn spent his summer and winter holidays in the Alps and alternate Easters with his Irish and English grandparents. His grandmother, a Kingsmill, was a gifted woman from whom his mother inherited a love of beauty in art and literature, as well as an appreciation of Catholicism. Like his parents, Arnold grew up approving of church unity, though this may have been because, with a Methodist father and Anglican mother, he sometimes had to attend church twice on Sundays.

At Easter 1893 Henry Lunn planned a visit to Rome, expecting to book 50 or 60 people. His company took 440 passengers. He knew Arthur Conan Doyle, who told him he was sick of Sherlock Holmes and wanted to kill him off so as to force people to take him seriously as a novelist. Henry took the writer to the Reichenbach Falls where the famous detective was to fall, apparently to his death. A couple of years later he was lecturing in New York and other cities in the United States and Canada,

Meanwhile, he had realised that to make money on his tours he must attract the wealthy, who would not travel with commoners. Although he had not been to public school himself, in 1903 he formed the Public Schools Alpine Sports Club, to assure his clients that they would travel only with people as rich and well educated as themselves. He himself had friends, like Herbert Asquith, in high places, and all this contributed to the success of his Club.

Henry Lunn booked whole hotels in his favourite resorts. Many places were well equipped with hotels and mountain railways for summer tourists. He persuaded the Swiss to keep the railways open in winter, so that his clients could use them to gain height for tobogganing, walking and eventually skiing.

So it was that Swiss resorts with mountain railways already built for summer, such as Murren, Wengen, and Zermatt, became the preferred destinations for British winter holidaymakers. The hotels were popular and sometimes fully booked, so a Swiss was once heard to complain to a receptionist: "You bloody boy, here I stand on Swiss bottom and cannot get a bed". Another story Arnold Lunn used to tell was of the King of the Belgians who, when visiting Murren said: "I would like my daughter to dance at the Palace, but perhaps it is against the rules. You see she was not educated at an English Public School."

In January 1903 Henry Lunn took his guests to Adelboden and organised the first ski race for a Challenge Cup open to British racers. The Public Schools Winter Sports Challenge Cup (later renamed the Public Schools Alpine Sports Club Challenge Cup) was then awarded based on the combined results of skiing, skating and toboganning. The first event was won by Arnold Lunn, then 14 years old.

Skiing gradually became accepted. In 1903 the Ski Club of Great Britain was founded. A small group of enthusiasts sat down to dinner at the Café Royal on 6 May and laid down the first rules of the Club. Its aims were: "To encourage ski sport generally, and in particular by the giving of information to members through the Secretary as to how, when and where to ski."

The first "Year Book of the Ski Club of Great Britain", published in 1905, mentions in a description of Adelboden: "Dr Lunn has hitherto engaged several of the hotels and filled them with his parties, which has, of course, added considerably to the number of sportsmen in Adelboden. He has now discontinued his patronage, which may make some difference in the number of visitors, but probably only to a slight extent."

The Lunn influence was already being felt in the Alps!

2

1902-8 Harrow and Balliol

True to the Public Schools tradition, in the late spring of 1902 Henry Lunn sent his son to Harrow. It was to give Arnold some fairly brutal early lessons in life and set him on a writing career. As a member of neither the aristocracy nor what he called the athletocracy, he developed an undeserved inferiority complex. In those days the captains of sport had their homework done for them by those who were better at lessons than sports. Lunn often rebelled against the accepted practices and, being stubborn, got kicked or beaten for his principles.

He showed no particular ability for sport and told of how he achieved success at squash only once, when he was playing with the school champion who told him to keep out of the court as much as possible. At Harrow's version of football, he was more interested in escaping the charge of the forwards than in taking the ball from them. He bought a diary in June 1904, which starts with a list of bets (mostly on cricket scores) and notes on who won and lost. But Harrow also encouraged his interest in literature and gave him a contempt for the unrealistic efforts of writers to capture the feelings of schoolboys.

At the age of sixteen he decided to write a school story himself. He began to write down in his diary the conversations of his friends. "My little friends soon discovered the diary and proceeded to 'review' my notes for a masterpiece by placing me in the centre of a critical circle and inviting all those mentioned in my works to boot my behind. Which they did. After that I persuaded my father to give me a diary with a Yale lock."

"The Harrovians", which he wrote about the school, was not published until 1913, when it was reviewed in The Times, Punch and The Manchester Guardian. Enthusiastically praised by some but violently attacked by others, it caused Lunn to be blackballed from several clubs. He had not written the book either to attack or reform Harrow, but because, he said: "Creation is as essential to the born writer as procreation to the lover."

There was no reason why he should attack Harrow. Though the early years were sometimes tough, he was not unsuccessful there and was sorry to leave. He ended as a monitor and head of his house, The Knoll, and he particularly enjoyed his last year. He wrote that he could think of no finer training for a young writer than to read his immature essays to George Townsend Warner. This Harrow master was the author of a brilliant book on the writing of English and was in some ways the most inspiring teacher he ever met. Harrow also formed the background of a novel, "Family Name", which was published in 1931.

At Harrow he acquired a classical education and was to baffle proofreaders later by including Greek quotations in his writings. He also learnt the importance of wit. He found he could protect himself against bullying by acting the clown. Like the medieval jester, he was expected to amuse the great and, when he succeeded, he enjoyed immunity from persecution. Much later he was to say that it was easier to persuade an audience or gain a point in a debate by making a joke rather than by reasoned argument. His father presented him with an ancient office typewriter to help him write. But the experiment of showing up with a hundred lines in the form of 25 typed lines and three carbon copies was not as successful as he had hoped!

The diary reveals his daily life and developing enthusiasms: "2nd August: had to go to London to be fitted for topper. 3rd August: sighted Alps about an hour before leaving Bern. Miss Coote met us at Interlaken. 6th September: Took two more photos of Mrs Marshal. Had a row with the Stationmaster. I was hanging onto a train and he hauled me off. Thanked him for saving my life and got fined 2 Francs. He offered me a quittance or receipt, which I told him to give to the kid to play with. In the evening met Mrs Marshal, very pretty."

The diary tells of many climbs with his brother Hugh in the holidays spent in the mountains, and at 16 he climbed his first real peak, the Aiguille de la Tour. "Our guide marched us methodically up to the summit and down to the valley again. A commonplace climb, and yet somehow few of my mountain memories are more enduring than the memory of my first night in a club hut, the first dawn I saw from the upper snows and the moment of my arrival on the summit of my first peak."

In 1905 he applied to become a member of the Ski Club of Great Britain, but was refused. It was to be 1910 before he was accepted as a member – to have a father occupied in "trade" was a barrier in those days. The clubs thought he would take advantage of membership to advertise his father's tours. But the SCGB was to play a major part in his life – and he was to play a major part in its achievements.

He spent three summers at Montana, which was no centre for an ambitious mountaineer but, with Hugh, Arnold explored the Wildstrubel-Wildhorn range without guides. They fell into crevasses and made all the traditional blunders, but they learnt to use rope and axe and acquired an eye for mountainous country and an instinct for route-finding.

To fill in the time at Harrow, he finished his first book "Guide to Montana", which described various routes up the Wildstrubel. He was helped by his fag to make the fair copy and the book was published in 1907, the year he left Harrow. When Donkin, one of the first really expert Alpine photographers, was killed in the Caucasus, his niece, Hilda, gave the enthusiastic young mountaineer a thousand of Donkin's prints. Lunn studied them and gained a very comprehensive knowledge of the scenery of the High Alps. Some time later he went to an Alpine Club exhibition with an old member. After Lunn had identified the locations of most of the photographs, the older man remarked: "You are surprisingly young to have done so much climbing", a compliment which Lunn received with mixed feelings, for at that time he had not even crossed the snowline.

He admitted that he could never remember dates in history, but never forgot the height of an Alpine peak. He had no difficulty in identifying any mountain, even far away, which he had once seen at close range, or of which he had seen a photograph. He found the changing aspects of the same peak full of significance to a mountain-lover. The Wetterhorn, for instance, seen from the Faulhorn, has a different personality from the same peak seen from the Scheidegg.

One summer day, many years later, he was walking with his wife, Mabel, through the Blumental at Murren, a valley full of wild flowers. When he criticised Mabel for not recognising a nearby peak, her answer was to pick a flower and ask him to identify it, which he could not do. Flowers did not arouse the same passion in him as mountains, which had an almost mystical effect on him. He wrote: "Suddenly I found myself asking whether matter alone, matter in the form of rock, ice and snow, could evoke the adoration which these mountains evoked in me."

Three weeks after leaving Harrow at 18 he was in Montana with Hugh. They had friends - two sisters called Helen and Cynara - staying nearby at Champex and planned to guide the girls up the Aiguille du Tour. The girls' mother, however, decided the boys were too inexperienced and arranged instead for the girls to go with a young Englishman, C. Scott Lindsay, who had two first-class guides. Scott Lindsay, born the same year as Arnold, had learned to ski while at the University of Freiburg.

The Lunn boys were so angry at this change of plan that they decided to get up early and catch up the party at the Cabane Dupuis. Unfortunately for Arnold, his sister Eileen's nurse, who was keeping a general eye on the whole family, took the precaution of hiding his climbing boots to prevent any such dangerous schemes. Undaunted, the boys set off, Arnold shod in thin English boots into which a few nails had been hurriedly inserted.

They slept at Sierre in the valley and left Martigny (480m) at 9am to climb to the Cabane Dupuis at 3,161m. Before starting to climb they had to trudge 8 miles along a dusty road. They reached the hut to find that the girls and Scott Lindsay, deterred by rain at midday, had not left Champex.

Next day the boys climbed the Aiguille du Tour, though the usual route was blocked by an enormous schrund. They only reached the pass between the two peaks by a steep slope of very hard ice, so steep that at one point Arnold had to cut handholds as well as footholds. One of his boots gave at the toe and he said some bitter things about his sister's governess. They reached the peak and descended to find their would-be companions still on their way to the Cabane Dupuis.

Scott Lindsay, who had a guilty conscience, gave a cry of alarm when he saw them and in mock terror hid behind a rock. However, they all went together to the Dupuis, including the girls' mother, who had never climbed before. Scott Lindsay had intended to ask the Lunn boys to join them on their climb, but the sight of Arnold's toe peeping through his boot put him off.

However, by 28 March the following year he wrote, rather formally, from Lausanne "Dear Mr Lunn", suggesting some climbs they might do together. They were to make many expeditions and he was to take an important decision for Lunn a few years later.

Things were not always easy for Henry Lunn at this time. He wrote to Arnold in August 1907 saying that it had been touch and go whether their boat, the Argonaut, would be ready in time for autumn cruises. If not, they would have lost £3,000. Fortunately it was ready in time.

School was followed by University and Arnold went up to Balliol for the Michaelmas Term of 1907. Balliol was a place for intellectuals and a hothouse for those who were to rule the country in the next generation. He made many friends, who were to have a great influence on his later life.

He might have done better academically had he attended to his lectures. Perhaps the reason he never achieved a degree was because he was said to have replied to a question about the social atmosphere of the court of James 1st: "No nice examiner would ever dream to set a question on this sordid theme". He was much more interested in philosophy, religion, science, poetry and his own writing than in compulsory subjects such as scripture, which he should have been studying. He did read a great deal, including Hilaire Belloc's "The Path to Rome", from which he took the idea that reason was the basis of faith.

Lunn was an agnostic, but up at Balliol at the same time was Ronald Knox, then a High Anglican who was to become a Roman Catholic and have a great influence on his life. Lunn was later to say that, of the Union Presidents in his day, Knox was outstandingly the most brilliant speaker. His wit always seemed spontaneous, however carefully he had prepared his speeches.

Lunn continued to climb during vacations and the following year, with Hugh and a guide called Biselx, he traversed the Aiguilles Dorees. Although suffering from food-poisoning (after eating tinned chicken for supper), they achieved the Tete Crettex, the Javelle, the summit of the Trident, the Tete Biselx (named after a relation of their guide) and made the traverse of the Aiguilles Penchees, up the Aiguille d'Argentiere and back by the Col du Chardonnet. Hugh returned to Germany, where he was learning the language. He too was writing, but under the name of Hugh Kingsmill because his father and brother already used the Lunn name. Arnold continued to climb each day, picking up companions, some of whom had never climbed before, which he called "pot luck mountaineering".

In January 1908, with a Mr Wyberg, he spent four days crossing the western wing of the Oberland range from Montana to Villars. They had sent a telegram to say they had arrived safely, but this went astray so search parties were sent out from Montana and Adelboden. After they left the telegram was delivered, so W.A.M. Moore and E. Russell Clarke of the Alpine Club set off and brought the searchers home.

Back at Oxford, Lunn went one evening as Knox's guest to hear a paper read on the Progressive Poets at the Shaftesbury Club. In his diary that evening he wrote that it was by accident that he spoke to Owen O'Malley. O'Malley said: "I first heard of you when a small party left to locate your corpse".

He invited Lunn to tea and they became friends. O'Malley went into the Diplomatic Service acting, in due course, as British Minister in Budapest and British Ambassador in Poland. It was in O'Malley's rooms at Magdalen that Lunn first suggested the foundation of a club for ski mountaineers. As he had been blackballed from the Ski Club of Great

Britain, it made sense to him to found his own club, which he called the "Alpine Ski Club". It included many of Lunn's friends, including W.A.M Moore and Scott Lindsay.

The aims of the Club were set out in the Annual, edited by Arnold Lunn in 1908, as: "To unite those bound by a common love for the mountains, joined to a desire to explore them in winter." It was not for those wanting to perfect their telemark turns, but to facilitate mountaineering on ski by fitting out club huts and publishing skiing guides. Lectures on skiing subjects and a journal containing the experiences of members were included in the Club's programme.

W.R. Rickmers, a German skier who had visited Zdarsky's Lilienfeld school and had also been present at the founding dinner of the Ski Club of Great Britain, was invited to become an Honorary Member of the Alpine Ski Club. He wrote to Lunn on 30 April 1908 from Samarkand, accepting the honour and congratulating Lunn: "That club is a necessity to form a counterweight to those rather conceited Ski Club of Great Britain people. You will easily get ahead of them by your business-like administration, for their last club tour to the Tyrol was shockingly mismanaged ".

In 1908 Lunn climbed the Matterhorn, funded by £10 made from the proceeds of his "Guide to Montana". In 1908 he also left Catania with a Mr Compton, drove up to Nicolosi, and from there climbed to the edge of the crater on Etna.

Meanwhile he continued to write and "The Alpine Ski Annual" appeared first in 1908 and was to be combined with "The British Ski Year Book" in 1920. "The Alpine Ski Guide to the Bernese Oberland" appeared in 1909. While at Oxford, he also founded the Oxford University Mountaineering Club, became Secretary of the Oxford Union, and the Editor of Isis.

The previous Editor of Isis, stung by a contemptuous reference to the undergraduates' weekly in an article by a former friend of Oscar Wilde, replied by a reference to his critic's "notoriously wilde manner". A libel action was threatened, damages were paid and the Editor was sacked. In the choice of a successor, the primary concern was to avoid further trouble and ensure that the next Editor should be both cautious and conciliatory. "That", said Lunn with tongue in cheek, "was why I got the job."

He also compiled "Oxford Mountaineering Essays," which was published by Edward Arnold in 1912. Lunn gave his friend Geoffrey Winthrop Young credit for the idea of this book and for "having inked cold daylight into more than one 'sunset' passage". His brother Hugh contributed, as did many of his friends including Julian Huxley and Norman Egerton Young. His own contribution was on "Roof-Climbing at Oxford" and included a fine account of climbing the Chapel.

"The Chapel – if you will allow a short excursion – is a good climb. It is best taken from the west. The heights once gained, there follows a spread-eagle traverse on a ledge past the clock (to resist setting its hands at sixes and sevens – if that metaphor be allowed – is hard). Thirty feet below are the flagstones of the quad. Next time you pass beneath the chapel arch, think of slow midnight figures shuffling along that narrow ledge above, feeling with anxious feet for the unseen, unpleasant wires, ridges and minor anfractuosities with which it is beset. From the ledge there is a press-up (without holds) onto the balustrade; what may be called the shoulder is now reached. The final pitch, a very interesting eastward-facing pipe, is left to climb; and then we are in the pure air of truth with mathematics and the rest of them."

Another essay he wrote was entitled "The Mountains of Youth" and headed by a fine poem by Geoffrey Winthrop Young. A signed copy of Young's book of poems "Wind and Hill", published in 1909, stayed with him all his life. The author became a friend and was godfather to Arnold's eldest son, Peter.

Lunn sent a copy of "Oxford Mountaineering Essays" to Hilaire Belloc, who wrote to thank him, saying he had been one of the original members of the Roof Club "in the beginning of time".

Because Lunn possessed an Alpine rope, his room came to be regarded as a useful route back to College after the gates were closed. He enjoyed the chance to be a roof climber and never forgot a sunrise after completing a somewhat hazardous first ascent: "Oxford had never seemed so beautiful. Her spires were silhouetted against the golden haze of a May dawn. And for the first time in my life, I felt that there were some things in England almost as lovely as the Alps."

"There are indeed three experiences in travel of which I never tire: the moment when the train sweeps out of the ravines of the Jura to reveal beyond the lake and beyond the green foothills the radiant gleam of the Oberland: the moment when one escapes from the ugly terminus at Venice to discover the Adriatic washing the station steps, and the turn in the railroad which discloses the spires of Oxford."

3

1909-13 Climbing and Marriage to Mabel

1909 was a crucial year. In January Lunn skied the first full traverse of the Bernese Oberland, from Kandersteg to the Grimsel; in April he met Mabel Northcote, who was to become his wife; he was sent down from Oxford and in August he suffered an injury that changed his life.

Henry Lunn opened Murren in winter that year to his clients. Walter Amstutz, who was then a small boy but was to become Arnold Lunn's greatest supporter in the battle for downhill racing, said the village was transformed overnight. The Alps were no longer out of season in winter. Murren quickly became fashionable. More English was spoken than Swiss German.

The Bernese traverse, described in "The Mountains of Youth" and "Come What May", began on 1 January in the company of Professor F. Roget of Geneva. Arnold Lunn wrote: "My father listened with sympathy to my schemes and made only one proviso: he insisted that I be accompanied not only by guides, but also by some experienced and elderly mountaineer. I accordingly invited Professor Roget to join me. He was an experienced climber, who had already accomplished some first-class ski expeditions, including the Grand Combin and the Aiguille du Chardonnet.

Although he had not learnt to ski before he was over 40, he was to achieve the first full traverse of the Haute Route to Zermatt in 1911.

Arnold Lunn was the only one in the party to use sealskins and Professor Roget was rather disparaging of this new-fangled invention. Until then skiers dipped their skis in water and placed them in the snow to form a coating of rough ice – a cumbersome and not very effective method of preventing skis slipping backwards downhill. The party engaged three guides of which one, called Adolphe, was described by Lunn as having "attained a degree of inefficiency unsurpassed in my experience."

They left Kandersteg at 5.30am bound for the Mutthorn Hut, which they did not reach until hours later. Their route led via the Petersgrat, Lotschental, Telli Glacier, Ried, Kippell, Lotschenlucke, Concordiaplatz, Grunhornlucke, Hugisattel, Finsteraarhorn, Fiesch Glacier, Oberaar Pass, Grimsel and Guttanen to Meiringen. It was a formidable achievement.

On 19 March Lunn went to Norway. The day he was leaving he rang Scott Lindsay to ask if he would go with him. "Of course I'll come" was the reply "but why the devil couldn't you tell me in reasonable time?" Lindsay left his office in the City, dashed home to Blackheath, packed and caught the afternoon train with Lunn.

They skied around Christiania (as Oslo was then called) and for a few days were joined by Canon Savage, another member of the Alpine Ski Club. Together they went to Fefor where they were rather irritated to find skiers wore evening dress for dinner. They were pleased, however, to see that the standard of skiing, except for a few experts, was well within the capabilities of the average English skier.

Lunn and Scott Lindsay went on to ski in Finse and together they crossed from Finse to the Hardanger Fjord. Cold and tired after the traverse and a steep descent to the fjord, they reached a little village, Ulvic, where they could have stayed the night. But Lunn had accepted an invitation from Canon Savage to spend a few days in Hexham. To reach there in time meant giving up the night's rest in Ulvic and spending two nights in an open sleigh, to catch the boat from Oslo. At some cost, the two men drove for eight hours that night and five hours across frozen lakes the next night. They caught the boat and Arnold Lunn kept his appointment.

He was to be rewarded for it was at Hexham that he first met Mabel Northcote. She was the daughter of the Reverend Hon. John Stafford Northcote, Chaplain to Her Majesty, and her brother Harry was later to become the Earl of Iddesleigh.

Her first impression of Arnold Lunn was not encouraging. She told her aunt that she had never met anyone like him in her life and hoped the experience would remain unique. But Lunn had been asked to lecture on mountains the next day and while she listened to him Mabel's opinion of the lecturer changed. That night she shared a room with a cousin, but she and Lunn managed to have a long conversation through the keyhole. At midnight, when he left after slipping a mountaineering journal under the door, he realised that it was 18 April and he had just come of age. Three days later, he proposed for the first time. Mabel was still not greatly impressed and after four proposals she gave him what he called "a definite conge".

Perhaps he had been too distracted from his studies by his climbs or his own writing, but when he returned to Oxford he found that he had been sent down. He had failed in the rudiments of Holy Scripture, an essential subject at that time. Henry Lunn fought on behalf of his son but without success. As long after as 30 November 1912, he was writing to The Master of Balliol College:

"You admit that the resolution under which Arnold was sent down was based upon the erroneous statement that he and Mr Primrose had failed twice, whilst Mr Primrose had failed twice and Arnold had only failed once. This is the vital point. There is no judge on the bench who, having misdirected the jury on false evidence, would sentence a man for any crime yet invented without allowing them the opportunity of revising their verdict when they knew the verdict was false.

It is not Arnold who is on his trial, but you and the Fellows of Balliol College for a gross injustice, which no body of men outside of the university would fail to condemn and which is indeed widely condemned in Oxford. I ask you again to cancel the entry of an unjust sentence and thus to some slight extent repair the wrong done."

It had no effect and Arnold Lunn regretted being sent down for several reasons. It was difficult to edit Isis away from Oxford; he was embarrassed at having to explain the lapse to his future father-in-law, Prebendary Northcote; and it spoilt his chances of becoming President of the Union, of which he had recently been elected Secretary. He complained too, that Scripture was a compulsory subject only to raise revenue for the university.

Soon after he was sent down, a review in praise of his articles in Isis appeared in the lady undergraduates' magazine. Intrigued, Lunn invited the reviewer, whose name was Joan Plowden, to tea and found that she too had been sent down. Lunn enchanted her with his epigrams; she enchanted him with her wit and beauty. When conversation lapsed he proposed to her and was afterwards to write that she had accepted him only to see what he would say. He said she was never in the least in love with him, but thought it would be fun to be engaged.

The engagement to Joan Plowden did not last long and though his absent-mindedness was often the cause of trouble, this was an occasion where it served him well. Lunn wrote two letters, one to a literary friend and the other to Mabel Northcote. In the first he gave a description of his fiancee with an invidious comparison between her and Mabel. Carelessly he put the letters in the wrong envelopes. When he discovered his mistake he was horrified, so wrote again to apologise to Mabel and subsequently called on her. A few weeks later Joan Plowden broke off the engagement.

Henry Lunn had decided that his son should become a barrister and encouraged him to study law. Arnold passed some of the bar exams, dutifully ate his dinners and described himself as an obscure member of the Inner Temple. But he was much more interested in his own writings than in studying law.

In August 1909 he decided to spend a few weeks writing a book in a little inn on the shores of Tallylyn in Wales. This is excellent rock-climbing country, which perhaps influenced his choice.

Certainly Scott Lindsay joined him for a few days of climbing, and on 28 August they climbed Great Gully, accompanied by a chance acquaintance, Mr Symes, who was there with a friend, Mr Warren. A casual remark revealed that Dick Warren was a rising surgeon on the staff of a London Hospital.

On the following day Lunn set off to walk up Cader Idris. Scott Lindsay did not feel like climbing, so Lunn left him and began to descend the east ridge of Cyfrwy. Judging by the standards of the day, the ridge was not difficult, but it has some steep pitches and a crack which, though short, has been compared with the famous 'Mummery Crack' on the Grepon.

The joy of that last unimpeded climb caused him later to produce some ecstatic prose: "The day was perfect. The burnished silver of the sea melted into a golden haze. Light shadows cast by scudding clouds drifted across the blue and distant hills. I slid down the crack and reached the top of the steep face of the rock above 'The Table'. The usual route dodges the top fifteen feet of this face and by an easy traverse reaches a lower ledge. But on that glorious afternoon I longed to spin out the joys of Cyfrwy and I found a direct route from the top to the bottom of this wall, a steep but not very severe variation ....I was glad to be alone. I revelled in the freedom from the restraints of the rope, and from the need to synchronise my movements with the movements of companions. I have never enjoyed rock-climbing more. I have never enjoyed rock climbing since. But at least the hills gave me of their best, full measure and overflowing, in those last few golden moments before I fell."

Scott Lindsay, who was admiring the view from Cader, was startled by the thunder of a stone avalanche. He turned to a nearby tourist, urging him to follow, and dashed off in the direction of Cyfrwy. Lunn described later what had happened: "I had just lowered myself off the edge of The Table. There was no suggestion of danger. Suddenly the mountain seemed to sway and a quiver ran through the rocks. I clung for one brief moment of agony to the face of the cliff. And then suddenly a vast block, which must have been about ten feet high and several feet thick, separated itself from the face, heeled over on top of me and carried me with it into space. I turned a somersault, struck the cliff some distance below, bounded off once again and, after crashing against the ridge two or three times, landed on a sloping ledge about seven feet broad. The thunder of the rocks falling though the hundred and fifty feet below my resting point showed how narrow had been my escape.

Fortunately, Scott Lindsay found him. Seeing Lunn's leg at an appalling angle, he dashed off to find Dick Warren, the surgeon, leaving the tourist who had come with him to look after the badly injured Lunn. However, the tourist did not stay long, saying that his wife was waiting for him. He left his cap to pillow Lunn's head and was to demand it back angrily the next day.

Scott Lindsay returned with help and took Lunn to hospital. Lunn's words to him from the stretcher were: "Do you think I shall ever climb again?" In the hotel at Dolgelly, where they had improvised an operating table, Dick Warren came to Scott Lindsay looking grave. In view of the dirty state of the wound and the time that had elapsed since the fall, it was strictly his duty to amputate the leg. He could only fail to amputate if a third party, responsible to the family, were to ask him to do so. Remembering Lunn's words from the stretcher and reflecting that Lunn without that leg would find life intolerable, Scott Lindsay took responsibility and Dick Warren did not amputate.

It was four months before Lunn left his bed and began to walk again, with the help of a splint. For the rest of his life the right leg was two inches shorter than the left. For eleven years bits of bone emerged from time to time from an open wound. The leg was slightly crooked but, thanks to the lucky meeting with Dick Warren and his immediate help, it was still what Lunn called very serviceable. He began to ski again fifteen months after the accident. But it was probably this injury that turned his energies from racing to organising ski races.

Scott Lindsay wrote to a Mrs Savage from the Angel Hotel, Dolgelly on Sunday 3 September: "I have been here with him since Tuesday and had joined him in some of his climbs. Today I didn't feel up to a climb and was walking up Cader Idris whilst he descended this ridge. Near the base of the rocks a big piece of rock broke away with him and he fell sheer almost 100ft. Mercifully he stopped on the edge of quite a narrow ledge, where we found him."

Lunn received many letters of sympathy, including one from Maudslie Castle Carluke: "I was proud to hear that your pluck and patience under the pain of being carried in were recognised as remarkable from J.L Steadill Davidson." Many ladies also wrote, including Geraldine Turpin and Mary Cadwalader Jones, who said: "I know how you hate to be fussed over."

Lunn was the last person to carry out the strict rules of antisepsis prescribed for the open wound. He was frequently told by doctors that TB or gangrene or some other serious infection would cost him the leg, but he insisted that, as he never bothered about antiseptics, he had built up an immunity.

Meanwhile, the Public Schools Alpine Ski Club thrived and Arnold continued to be involved in his father's business. He spent the summer after his accident at Garmisch-Partenkirchen in Germany.

The Ski Club of Great Britain accepted him as a member in 1910, but the most prestigious mountaineering club of the time was the Alpine Club and that was still barred to him because of his connection with his father's company. Henry Lunn was awarded a knighthood in 1910 for "Services to Anglo-German Relations." He had worked with Germans and met the Kaiser.

On 6 January 1911 Arnold and his father organized a race at Montana, above Sierre, which is now recognized as the first modern downhill. Ten racers competed, among them Arnold's brother Brian. C.N. Buzzard, another competitor, wrote about it in the 1949 British Ski Year Book.

They left Montana at 1,471m and climbed for seven-and-a-half hours to spend the night at 2,700m in the Wildstrubel Hut on the Plaine Morte glacier. On the day of the race they climbed into a high wind, which was blowing up the frozen snow into a kind of blizzard. Buzzard was 38, far older than most of the others. At 10am they all started together and raced for about thirty minutes across the glacier and then some 1,524m down over untracked snow to a point before Montana. Arnold, prevented from racing by his injury, was standing about 350m from the finish when Cecil Hopkinson, the subsequent winner, arrived. Hopkinson stopped there and had a drink which, to judge from Lunn's contemporary account, did not strike him as unusual. The winning time was 61 minutes.

Lord Roberts of Kandahar, hero of the Afghan War, had agreed to be first Vice-President of the Public Schools Alpine Sports Club and also let his name be given to the cup awarded to the winner. So the race became known as the Roberts of Kandahar. Lord Roberts was not at the race but had visited Montana recently, and had probably been persuaded to give the cup by Lord Lytton. That was how the name Kandahar, coming from Afghanistan, became famous in the world of skiing.

In January 1911 Mabel started skiing at Grimmi Alp. On her fourth day on skis, she went on a tour with Arnold and two others. They climbed 750 m and skied down. She arrived at the finish somewhat exhausted, but still game, and became engaged to Lunn a few days later.

Lunn's enthusiasm for ski mountaineering remained strong, even after his climbing accident. In 1911 he climbed the Dent Blanche from Zermatt. In "Mountains of Memory", published in 1948, he was to describe a climb made at the end of January 1912. "I left Murren for England. I was reading for the Bar and there were dinners to be eaten and examinations to be passed, but there was something repulsive about the look of the departure platform at Basle, something curiously charming about the platform from which trains start for Bern. Murmuring to myself "second thoughts are best", I jumped aboard. In Murren, Edward Tennant was about to set out on the first winter ascent of the Lauterbrunnen Breithorn. The two men walked down to Stechelberg and Lunn achieved the climb – on two ropes – despite doubts about whether his bad leg would stand up. By this time he had spent seventeen summers and eleven winters in the Alps.

A row in the British ski establishment caused the founding of the British Ski Association in June 1912, and on 13 August 1912 the National Ski Union was founded. Then on 28 November 1913 a meeting was held of the United Ski Council, to which the SCGB and the BSA sent representatives and they agreed it was to be the supreme skiing authority.

Lunn deserted the Bar before taking his finals because the success of his book "The Harrovians" encouraged him to believe that he could make a living as a writer. He continued to edit Isis for some time. "Guide to Montana" had already been published and "Oxford Mountaineering Essays" appeared in 1912. "An Englishman in the Alps", a collection of English prose and poetry, was to follow in 1913. Lunn sent a copy to Mabel, commemorating their engagement and inscribed: "Mabel Stafford Northcote from Arnold Lunn, January 16 1913 (dies dierum)."

"Skiing" also appeared that year, and included chapters on equipment, techniques for beginners (the telemark was recommended as the best way to turn), ski-mountaineering, where to ski, routes in the High Alps, and recollections from his own experiences. He ended with a fine tribute: "We, whose physical disabilities cut us off from the enjoyment of other sports, can never be too grateful that even the halt may sometimes pass the silent gateways of the snows."

There was useful travel information in the book, including the fact that the fare by the shortest rail route to Gstaad was £9 10s 6p for a First-Class Return. The horse-drawn sleigh ride from Frutigen to Adelboden took 3 hours.

Writing was his real vocation and he combined it with taking groups of his father's clients on tours. He also commented on ladies skiing – obviously influenced by the petite and competent Mabel:
"Skiing is admirably adapted to the physique of the average woman. It does not involve sudden spurts of ferocious energy. The labour of the ascent is not concentrated into brief spasms of effort but is evenly spread over a long

interval. If the lady runner has mastered the correct style, her skiing will be free and effortless. The sport does not involve ungainly attitudes. A lady playing hockey is a strangely unaesthetic object, but the same woman on ski may easily prove more graceful and attractive than in any other role. Ladies, more often than not, possess the nerve and dash essential to brilliant ski running."

But later in the same book he wrote: "On mountaineering, of course, they are quite outclassed by men, and when we hear of ladies transposing 'the most difficult climb in the Alps' into an 'easy day for a lady' it is as well to remember that every expedition made by a lady is led by a man. Til ladies begin to carry out severe guideless climbs without masculine assistance, they cannot be considered in the same class with a good man mountaineer. Nonetheless, they made very good seconds on the rope.

As a rule they show greater pluck and give less trouble than men when things go wrong, chiefly because they retain to the last a touching, if misplaced, confidence in the male members of the party. I have been in more than one nasty experience in the Alps with ladies and I have been profoundly thankful for their courage and unfailing cheerfulness.

Where ladies so often fail is in want of imagination. Without wishing to intrude on controversial ground, I think most mountaineers would agree that women have less imagination than men. A man knows as he packs his knapsack after breakfast, he will feel hungry higher up. A girl in similar circumstances cheerily assures you that three biscuits, a bar of chocolate and an apple will suffice for a 3-hour run. Similar arguments will convince her that spare gloves and a woollen helmet are unnecessary additions to her sack. Later they either turn to you for assistance or, from a foolish striving after a consistency which no one expects from their sex, decline food and garments, thus risking faintness and frostbite."

To today's feminists this may display a maddening mixture of condescension and consideration, but in his day Lunn was more liberal than most men in dealing with what was then known as 'the fair sex'. In a world where they were considered unintelligent and weak, he was the first to acknowledge that they also had their strengths. He often referred with pride to Mabel's skiing and he approved of lady judges when other members of the club sought to exclude them.

Lunn wrote often to his mother, who must have worried about her son after he had been sent down from Oxford and then gave up the Bar. However, on 2 August 1913 she wrote to him from the Grand Hotel at Le Zoute: "My darling Arnold, the only thing I really care about is that my children have an ideal and try to reach it. You have now admitted that you had such in writing the Harrovians and I am quite content. More than that, I feel you have shown great courage." Arnold took after his father in one important direction. He said his father was never happier than when he was one of a minority. They both enjoyed a fight.

In the summer of 1913 Mabel stayed with the Lunn family at Murren and Arnold took her up the Lobhorn, which in those days ranked as a difficult rock climb. He wrote of her that, except that she lacked strength, she had every qualification for rock climbing and skiing. She certainly had plenty of courage and a perfect balance. She was always fragile and easily tired and, if she had not had an iron will, she would never have passed the Ski Club of Great Britain's third-class test, let alone the first-class.

Her father died before he could inherit the title of Earl of Iddesleigh, but Mabel and her sister were awarded the title Lady when their uncle inherited the Earldom.

On 10 December 1913 Arnold and Mabel were married. Geoffrey Winthrop Young was Best Man (and almost eclipsed the bridegroom with the splendour of his clothes). After a few days in the south of France, they left for Switzerland and spent a fortnight at the Palace Hotel in Wengen.

One perfect January morning they took the train to the Jungfraujoch and set off for the Jungfrau. The summit was icy that day and they roped up. Arnold was reshaping the steps cut by a previous party when suddenly he stepped clean out of the rope. The noose had worked loose. There was an angry hiss of the rope darting down like a snake. It jerked at Mabel's waist, but she stood firm in her ice steps. Arnold never forgot the horror of the moment. They climbed the Monch together before returning to Wengen. This was Mabel's first peak – for they had not completed the ascent of the Jungfrau – and her last. She much preferred skiing to mountaineering – not surprising after such experiences.

Mabel was tiny, less than 5ft tall, with golden hair and an effervescent personality. A beautiful dancer, described as "light as thistledown", she was also great fun. There is no doubt that she added greatly to the social side of Murren life in the golden years of the 'twenties and thirties', when skiers packed evening dresses with their ski trousers and dancing at night followed skiing by day. Fancy-dress balls were a feature of each season.

The Lunn's first home was "Suttoncroft" at Cookham in Kent, which they loved, and their first landlord was Sir George Young, brother of Geoffrey Winthrop Young.

After Mabel Lunn's death, Phyllis Holt-Needham, who knew her well, was to write: "Mabel was essentially an individualist both in her own life and tastes and in her approach to other people. Of the hundreds of men and women she would meet during the year, she remembered always small personal details, generally connected with ways in which she could do something for them. She combined a penetrating understanding of other people's problems with a fundamental reticence in her approach to them. She did not probe or sit in judgement and she never seemed to expect more than people were prepared to give. I find it impossible to describe her humour, which was such a delight to her friends. She had a wonderful sense of timing and it was the occasion of her pointed, often deflationary witticisms that one remembers, not the words she used."

Meanwhile, Lunn applied himself to writing. In 1913 he edited "The Climbers Club Journal" and the "Alpine Ski Club Annual". "Skiing" was published by Eveleigh Nash and in it he gave advice to the beginner on equipment, clothes, technique and where to ski. That year also he started "The Alps" for the Home University Library and finished it in March 1914. It traced man's involvement with the Alpine chain, its exploration and the literature it inspired.

4

1914-18 WORLD WAR I & AFTER

Just before the war Lunn's leg was allowing him – though often with intense pain – to continue ski-mountaineering. In June 1914 he had an action-packed week that would have taxed any fully-fit man.

He left London on a Wednesday and spent Friday skiing near the Jungfraujoch; on Saturday he climbed the Fiescherhorn on ski; on Sunday he skied down to the Eggishorn and slept at Fiesch; on Monday he made his way to the Betemps Hut; on Tuesday he climbed Monte Rosa, went back to sleep that night in Bern and arrived back in London next day.

It was decided in 1914 to unite the various British ski clubs, to coordinate their tests and publish a single magazine instead of each club having its own. So the United Ski Council became the Federal Council of British Ski Clubs. On 30 June, Frank Trier, Honorary Secretary and Treasurer of the Ski Club of Great Britain, wrote to the Chairman of the Federal Council at 18a Cannon Street. He notified him that his Committee appointed F.G. Fedden and Kenneth Swan to represent the SCGB on the Council and that any of the elected members of the committee of the SCGB were eligible to serve on the Federal Council as substitutes as and when required. Fedden, who was the SCGB's President, was elected Chairman of the Council for the first year and remained in place until 1920 because of the war. The first meeting was held on 2 July 1914 and the Council continued until 1925.

When war was declared Lunn tried to join the army, but was immediately turned down because of his injured leg. He spent the first three months cursing because he was out of it all. He had no great desire to kill Germans, but wanted to see their Prussian leaders defeated. He wrote: "I never did like the Prussian. He is too much like my own countrymen, but the old Bavarian is an excellent fellow and the average Bavarian peasant has more culture in his little finger than the average Englishman has in his whole body."

He travelled out through France to Switzerland and back again between 24 August and 2 September 1914 and the sight of the soldiers going to war and the wounded returning depressed him. He did his best to help repatriate his injured countrymen and visited a great many Swiss hoteliers. He also tried to get a job with the Quaker ambulance units out in France. He hoped to make things easier for the wounded, but came back to England rather disillusioned.

On 14 November, to Arnold Lunn's great delight, Mabel gave birth to a son, Peter. He inherited his father's love of skiing and became a very successful racer, as well as a convinced Roman Catholic and an accomplished author.

Early in January 1915 Arnold Lunn drove to The Atholl, Pitlochry, in a motorcycle and sidecar, which he said "simply skied down" on the ice. Vivian Caulfeild, who shared his interest in ski technique and had written a book entitled "How to Ski" in 1911, came to join him. The two men reflected on hotels. Why was it, they wondered, that the Swiss and foreigners do not realise the importance of making their guests feel at home and comfortable and that the English only do so in hotels provided with German waiters?

A few days later he went to Dalwhinnie, where Mabel had arrived with Peter. They met members of the Scottish Ski Club and enjoyed being among "ski-runners" again. In March he skied for three days. Mabel came with him one day and they had good practice in telemarks and jumping around. On 22 April he was back again in Moffat. "I am here without

Mabel, who has basely deserted me and gone off to Quetta. I don't like it much. Mabel looks after me so well. The ghost of Bachelor Arnold feels vaguely that something is amiss. Bachelor didn't notice when he wasn't comfortable, but Ghost does. Bachelor doesn't mind leaving things untidy, but Ghost doesn't like to find them untidy. Bachelor hates unpacking for himself and putting things in drawers. Ghost is pained at the amount of litter that collects. Ghost knows that he ought to sort this out and that Mabel would make him sort it out, but Ghost lets things drift and gets thoroughly uncomfortable. On the other hand, Ghost wears untidy soft collars, which is some slight consolation."

His affection for Peter is shown in constant references. "Peter is getting a very fine baby. He is a very thorough egoist and likes your complete unflagging attention. If he doesn't get this he howls. If he does, he sometimes laughs and coos and this is not a bad reward for one's trouble."

Caulfeild came to visit them and cut ski from cardboard and made them run on wheels to demonstrate that steering is quite sufficient to bring off a Christiania and a Telemark. When the men didn't meet they corresponded about how to ski. Lunn complained that he had to send Caulfeild a stamped envelope and a piece of writing paper and even occasionally a pencil in order to receive a letter four months later. Caulfeild resolutely refused to have anything to do with the war, so Lunn wrote and told him he was glad to see that he was still sticking to 'his guns'. He had not stopped writing and was struggling with a novel called "The Peculiar Friendship". Finally, he decided to give it a rest for a bit as he did not think it the kind of novel for wartime. People want something light. So he searched for an interim potboiler and eventually abandoned his first manuscript.

He missed Switzerland, saying: "Nowadays I can read the veriest rot about Switzerland with real pleasure. It's like being back at school, when the sight of Switzerland on a map made me feel homesick. There is not a minute of the day when I do not think of the Alps and long for Switzerland." He did manage to go to Switzerland though in the summer of 1915, visiting

Wengen, Bern, Montreux and Villars, then travelling via Zurich to Chur, Lenzerheide and back to Wengen, always dealing with hoteliers and discussing the effects of war.

From Wengen he managed a day on the Jungfraujoch. "I shall never forget the run down from the Joch. Barring the pulver schnee of January, I have never had anything much better. The snow had just reached the intermediate stage between soft wet snow and firm crust. And I did go fast! I was running very well indeed, quite on top of my form. It is just about 2,000ft, perhaps a little less, from the Joch to the foot of the Trugberg. Walkers on foot are lucky if they get down in an hour and a half - I took just eight minutes. The wind shrieked in my ears and the crisp cutting sound of my ski driving through the soft immature crust was wholly delightful. It was great fun jumping small crevasses a few inches wide and at the top of my speed I darted down onto a crevasse about seven feet broad and cleared it without falling, a wonderful sensation."

He managed a notable climb, leaving the Concordia Hut with a companion to climb the Gletscherhorn. It proved difficult and they had to spend a night out in the snow, but Lunn's leg coped with some very tough going.

His knowledge of snowcraft often saved his life. Rather than relying on the experience of guides, he regarded them as partners in a common enterprise. When he climbed with them, he reserved the right to plan the tour and make the trickier decisions about snowcraft himself. More than once he had been led towards a dangerous situation which, with the handicap of his bad leg, would have led to his death.

Twice he reached Alpine peaks alone because his companions dared not or could not follow. One complained that he was: "cosmopolitan and urbane below the snowline, but degenerated rapidly into un vrai type Anglo-Saxon in the High Alps."

Henry Lunn, who knew Herbert Asquith well, was a frequent visitor to No. 10 Downing Street. Henry and Mabel went to an Asquith family wedding, but Arnold had a bad headache and cried off.

His sister-in-law Eileen visited them for a couple of days and they all had a séance with a Mrs Hoare. Lunn was always interested in - though sceptical about - spiritualism, but he said Mrs Hoare talked utter balderdash. They sat in darkness for two hours and he said he gave the damned spirits every chance. The table creaked once or twice and did an occasional spasmodic jerk, but nothing more than that. It did not convince him.

Arnold and Mabel spent a fortnight in Scotland at the end of October, mainly in Pitlochry. On 14 November Arnold was remembering Peter's birth a year before: "Then he was very red and bald and squeely. Today he is really a very good-looking little ruffian with curly hair and a most bewitching smile. He will shake hands when required to and salute whether required to or not. Damn will have to disappear from my vocabulary for it would never do to have him saying dam dam instead of da da. Will he have Switzerland as a background for his childhood? I hope so. Will he like the things that are worth liking? I wonder. Or will he react from me as I reacted from my father and develop into a curate, blameless and worthy?"

He saw a lot of Hugh and Eileen when in Britain. Hugh was expecting to be sent to the Dardanelles to fight, and gave Arnold instructions in case he did not return. But at the last moment he was sent into Intelligence instead. Arnold went with him to Waterloo and was in London during the Zeppelin raids on 15 November.

The brothers discussed religion and when the conversation turned to the Trinity, Lunn said: "As a consistent radical I could not bring myself to prostrate before Christ. He may have been the Son of God, but that is no reason why I should grovel before him. He owes his position to a mere accident of birth."

Cecil Chesterton was lecturing on "The Prussian hath said in his Heart" to an audience composed in the main of the Catholic Association. After the lecture he went for a whisky and soda to the Lunn's house at Suttoncroft and reminded Arnold that his more famous brother, G.K. Chesterton, had been asked to lecture at Balliol when Arnold was Secretary of the Union.

Henry Lunn was running a campaign against The Times. His idea was to get a number of prominent men to sign a document pledging themselves never to write for the paper. Arnold tried to dissuade him saying that they gave him occasional work and reviewed his books well. The Times had also been useful to the family business in reporting on their events. "My rule," Arnold said, "is that every new enemy is a luxury." There was a family connection too, for Hubert Walter, whose family ran The Times, had married Mabel's first cousin.

Finally, Lunn found some war work for which he was very well suited. The Swiss Government had generously arranged to intern prisoners of war who were suffering from certain specified diseases and disablements. By 1916 this agreement was extended to all officers and NCOs who had been in Germany for more than two years. Camps were set up in Montreux, Montana, Chateau d'Oex and Murren. Lunn, used to arranging accommodation for his father's clients, was sent to organise them.

He and Mabel went out first to Montana, which was to be used for wounded French officers. Lunn was thrilled at the opportunity to see the mountains again and to ski. He looked forward to "the Sun athwart slopes of deep powder snow, each crystal snowflake a separate Sun. With such a lot of misery in the World one is almost ashamed of such happiness."

They left Charing Cross on 18 January 1916, travelling via Paris. Marcel Kurz, a ski-mountaineering friend, appeared in the train to Pontarlier to talk to them. The Lunns set up the organisation for the reception of the French. There was a great deal of administration to arrange, which was complicated by the health of the prisoners. The Lunns then went on, via Montreux, to Murren. Together with baby Peter and an English nanny, they lived at first in a little chalet in Murren.

Mabel was to suffer a terrible year. In May 1916 her brother Hugh was killed at the Front. On 19 September came the news that her brother Teddy had also been killed. Teddy, heir to the Earldom, had held the German third line with six men for several hours and refused several messages telling him to come back if he wished to. He fought in a number of German dugouts full of men before being killed. Then Mabel's father was diagnosed as having cancer. Even the nanny they liked so much died in February.

During 1916 about 28 officers and 500 NCOs and men arrived in Murren. Lieut-Colonel Neish of the Gordon Highlanders was appointed as Senior British Officer and the disciplinary and medical arrangements were made by the Swiss. Captain Dr, Pedro Llopart was their Commanding Medical Officer. The organisation was considerable, for tailors, shoemakers, carpenters and barbers shops were set up in the various resorts by the Red Cross in Bern. The men were taught French, German, Spanish, Russian, bookbinding, woodcarving and typewriting.

In April 1916 Lunn was reporting that in three months he had learned a prodigious amount of German, written a good deal, started on geology and read many books including Balzac and Maupassant. He also did some spring skiing and studied snow conditions. He found snow does not stick once thoroughly thawed, though it may be a bit slow with the Sun full on it. He learnt that it is usually best to choose south-facing slopes after the Sun has set, and north-facing slopes in the heat of the day. South slopes, which avalanche most readily in winter, are comparatively safe in spring and north slopes become increasingly dangerous as the year advances. But even south slopes are safe when the Sun has set, provided always that a warm wind is not blowing and that the slopes are steadied by frost.

On 15 April he toured from Zinal to Zermatt with Joseph Knubel, making a detailed itinerary of times, routes, etc. Going up the Rothorn, they dragged their skis by string fastened to their rucksacks, and found they went up 1,000m of steep hard snow very easily. Lunn forgot suncream for his face and burnt very badly. They crossed from Trifthorn to Zermatt and advised against their route to the top of the Trifthorn.

On 18 April he celebrated his 28th birthday with some philosophical thoughts: "Moments of divine beauty …make me hunger for some hint of permanence in the Universe, for some hope that somewhere, somehow, I shall wake again and see the glory of other springs long after my body forms the soil from which spring flowers rise. When I first began to doubt, at the age of 18, I used to search the works of Agnostics with a desperate longing to find that even they believed in some purpose in the Universe, … I care nothing for the philosophy of Christianity, and the traditional theory of the incarnation of an omnipotent God who invents evil to vary the monotony of good and then has to send his own son to be crucified so as to save from his own damnation the creatures he has mismade, seems to me both silly and unsatisfactory. But I do care intensely that the Universe should mean something and that all achievement should have some permanent value."

To keep his charges fit, Lunn arranged ski lessons (they learnt the stem turn) and tests for both officers and men. The tests were run according to new rules, which had been worked out by the Federal Council in the spring and summer of 1914. They formed a valuable testbed for discussions after the war. Letters to Vivian Caulfeild discussed the abolition of stick riding and the choice of a single stick or two.

Lunn organised many ski tours for the better skiers, in the course of which they climbed various minor peaks such as the Ebnefluh, and crossed the classic glacier passes. They went from Murren to the Concordia Hut via the Jungfraujoch and made an ascent of the Mittaghorn with a run down to Goppenstein. Not all of his charges, however, took to skiing, which seemed too much like hard work to most of them. "What use is skiing to the British working man?" asked one.

There were occasional days of joy in the mountains, but there were many more of hard work, making sure that food and medical supplies were adequate and keeping the peace. In a constant stream of letters home, Lunn told of parleying between doctors, caterers and men. In one letter from Montana, he wrote: "I have sacked the cook for drunkenness". There were always problems over accommodation. Lunn liaised with Colonel Neish and did his best to mediate in the occasional differences between him and the hotel management.

In a typical letter dated 4 November 1916, Lunn reported: "My Dear Father – Just back from Montreux and Chateau d'Oex. Costs had risen as the doctors were prescribing special rations for the men." On 23 November he was writing: "We are expecting 155 men, 20 officers in two or three days. Mabel and I went down to Bern to attend the wedding of one of the officers. Butter and potatoes are hard to get."

Frequent, friendly letters were also exchanged with his brothers Brian and Hugh. To his mother he wrote about his recreations and especially about Mabel and Peter. In December 1916 he wrote to his mother: "Three or four times a week I take out skiing parties of officers, NCOs and men. This is a job which requires great patience and some little tact. You have so many people to deal with. There are the Swiss, the somewhat swollen-headed Dr Llopert, the Colonel, the officers, the officers' wives. Pods against Presbyterians, Regular Officers against one or two Canadian officers; one spends all one's time humouring people one would like to kick, or having violently to sit on people one rather likes."

He was learning diplomacy as he dealt with British soldiers, Swiss administrators and local villagers. "If you give in gracefully over a number of little points, they forget that you have not given in over the big one".

In a letter to his brother Brian, dated 15 December, he discussed the rival beauty of various resorts. "I read your letter about Montana versus Murren and it interested me. I think I agree. Montana is certainly much lovelier than Murren, but Murren has a touch of the old Grindelwald sort of Switzerland, which is bound up with a lot of things one likes. It is more Echt Schweiz. Montana has a suggestion of Italy, very pleasing. I remember the night I heard about Teddy, I was at Sierre". Mabel wrote to Arnold while he was away in Montana, that Peter who was with her was "a radiant little being, like you, but sturdier. His observation is quite remarkable."

The winters at Murren during the war proved to be rich in snow. In 1916 excellent skiing was enjoyed from the middle of October to the middle of May 1917 and that year the winter set in as early as 5 October. By the middle of that month, deep and excellent powder was to be found all round Murren.

Lunn made some good friends among the military and his happiest memories were of skiing over the Oberland glaciers with three officers: Ralph Evans, Bob Middleditch and E.T.R. Carlyon. A most important friendship forged in the war was with Walter Amstutz, the Murren boy whose parents ran the Alpina Hotel on the brink of the cliffs. Born in

1902, Walter had been to school first in Murren, then in Lauterbrunnen, 850m below. Henry Lunn had not then persuaded the Swiss to run their mountain trains in winter, so the young Walter, with his school friends, would get up at 5.30am, ski down to Lauterbrunnen and climb back in the evening when school was over. He was to prove an expert in both slalom and downhill and became a staunch supporter in the battle for their recognition.

From 1928 to 1938, Amstutz was Tourism Director of St Moritz, where he invented speed skiing, setting up a flying kilometre. He designed the Sun logo for the resort. An expert mountaineer, he climbed with King Albert of the Belgians, whom he met at a prize-giving for Anglo-Swiss races. Through the Kandahar, he also met Prince Chichibu and became a connoisseur of Japanese prints. He was to run a fine-arts printers, the De Clivo Press, and to assemble a notable collection of paintings.

Sir Henry Lunn was caught up by the intense anti-German feeling in Britain and was attacked in the Press for being pro-German. He fought a long court case to clear his name and eventually got apologies and costs from three Scottish papers, and most of his costs from the Morning Post. Mrs Asquith sent him a letter of sympathy.

Arnold and Mabel refused presents that Christmas because they said they were so well off in Switzerland. For a time they were worried about Brian, who was in the Tigres push but survived. He was taken ill in Mesopotamia and was invalided out of the Army, from which he went into the Colonial Office for the rest of the war. Hugh was taken prisoner and wrote a book called "Behind Both Lines". In it he showed the same realism and dry wit as Arnold: "I thought of my men. How they would fail to miss me!"

Occasionally there were opportunities to escape from duties and enjoy some ski-mountaineering. In June 1917, with Joseph Knubel, Lunn made the first ski ascent of the Dom, the highest point accessible on ski in Switzerland. Lunn had given Knubel his first pair of skis years before and the Swiss was now an experienced guide. The mountain had been climbed before on foot, but this time they were determined to make ski tracks to the very top. They set out on 16 June, with Rudolf Lechmatter as porter, and rested at the Festi Hut. As he smoked peacefully, Lunn reflected that from no point in the Alps can the Weisshorn be more beautiful. They started next morning at 5am and cut the first ski track to the summit of the Dom at 11.30.

Lunn was trying out new short skis, not unlike the "compacts" produced much later. One of the pair he used still hangs in the Ski Club of Great Britain's clubhouse. It is only 1.6m long and was described by him as a short summer ski. A hole in the front shows how it was hauled up the steeper stretches of the mountain by a cord. He found their lightness a great advantage when climbing.

The slopes they negotiated were "abominably steep", so they studied the texture of the snow to make sure it would not avalanche. Fortunately Lunn was able to describe it as: "like powder snow in winter that has been caked up by wind". With some care they reached the top and spent half an hour enjoying their success on the windless summit. Then they set off down on ski. For the first 60 metres the snow was still dangerously unstable, but the rest was pure joy. Their running time for the descent, not counting two halts and a rock traverse, was only 40 minutes.

Still interested in religion and sceptical about Roman Catholicism, Lunn wrote one day to his mother from the Palace Hotel in Murren: "There is an Irish Priest here and I was interested to know how far the strict Catholic position clashes with geology. Apparently you can concede seven very long days for creation – several thousand years – but my little priest would have nothing of Darwinism and insisted that Genesis was history from start to finish. I felt a sort of satisfaction that Catholics are pinned down to such an untenable position for I do not like the Catholic view of religion. He, poor man, had a gleam in his eye which all Catholics have when you ask them about their peculiar creed – the gleam that means: 'This heretic is getting interested. It's the first step'."

Ronald Knox, who had been at Balliol with Lunn, was received into the Catholic Church in 1917 and wrote a book describing his conversion, entitled "A Spiritual Aeneid", which appeared in that year. It annoyed Lunn and provoked him into writing a satirical essay, which he was not successful in getting published. Finally, he wrote "Roman Converts", a study of five eminent converts to the Catholic Church: Newman, Manning, Chesterton, Tyrell and Knox. He was to spend three years writing it and was convinced that the Roman position was untenable – but his conviction was cracking. Gradually, he was making Catholic friends such as G.K Chesterton and Hilaire Belloc. Like Belloc, his religious convictions were strong and his religious feelings weak.

In 1918 he tried to put an aluminium running surface on to the bottom of a pair of skis. Five friends went out together, two on ordinary skis, two with skis coated with aluminium, and one with copper. It was not a success. The aluminium peeled off very quickly and the metalised skis stuck to the snow more easily than the ordinary ones. They also proved heavier than ordinary skis. It was not until after the second world war, during which Donald Gomme learnt about bonding metal and wood in an aircraft factory, that the very successful bonded Gomme skis were made.

In the last winter of the war, Lunn achieved a marathon five days of ski-mountaineering with his friends. On the Monday they climbed the Kleine Scheidegg, a total climb and descent, including the re-ascent from Grund, of 1,230m. On the Tuesday they climbed the Lauberhorn (1,640m), on Wednesday the Schwarzhorn (1,873m) on Thursday the Wildgerst (1,835m) and skied down 2,283m to Meiringen. After a day's rest, they traversed the Faulhorn to Meiringen by the long route and this involved about 2,440m of climbing and 2,900m of downhill skiing. Lunn said he never really felt tired, but for a man with an open break still affecting his right leg it was a remarkable achievement.

On 22 January 1918 he was still reflecting on Roman Catholicism, which he rejected: "I feel convinced I shan't end up a Catholic, whatever happens. I rather fancy I shall end up a believer in the old Greek religion with its fine assortment of Gods so much more interesting than the monotheism they supplanted. There was some colour in their religion, by Jove!"

He said that as a child he had thought that if God were omnipotent, then why should we go to church and ask his help to convert heathens. Also, when he was about 8 he had asked a lady whether people who refused to believe in Christ would go to Hell. He was told they would, but that if they had not been told of Christ they would be saved. In that case, he decided, if there were no missionaries all heathens would go to Heaven. If there were missionaries, some heathens would go to Heaven and others to Hell.

Henry Lunn's secretary, Dora Jones, gave friendly advice to Arnold, who often sent her and his father, as well as his brother Brian, chapters of the books he was writing for their comments. When Hugh was taken prisoner Arnold wrote to him, giving what news he could. On 22 September 1918 he wrote: "Brian is becoming an awful bug at the Colonial Office. Quite the complete mandarin".

He heard that Joan Plowden was engaged to a French Officer and told Hugh: "I have written to congratulate her. I hope I shall draw a reply. I should like to meet her again. She was a very lively young woman." He sent his ex-fiance a long friendly letter, recalling happy times, regretting that they had parted in anger and hoping her marriage would be as happy as his.

Although he was able to enjoy some days of ski touring, the job of looking after so many interned soldiers required a lot of work. New drafts from Germany were often delayed and budgets were difficult to keep to. Lunn said he was constantly accused of swindling the officers who were housed in the luxury of the Palace. For 7 Swiss Francs they were getting accommodation and food, for which in normal times they would have had to pay anything from 15 to 25 Swiss Francs a day. He was always travelling between the various resorts. It was a huge relief when finally the war was over.

5

1919-24 The Golden Years

THE INTERNED LEFT Murren for home on 20 December 1918, and Lunn too was able to return to England. On 19 January 1919 he boarded the steamer at Romanshorn and said goodbye to Switzerland. He was travelling with George Young, the owner of Suttoncroft and brother of Geoffrey Winthrop Young, the mountaineer who had been Best Man at his wedding.

George Young was in the Diplomatic Service and had managed to smuggle a precious trunk containing food through three frontiers. Lunn left it behind at Lindau, where Young had to rescue it. This was early evidence of the absentmindedness that was to dog him throughout his life. He himself said he was "present minded – concentrating so much on whatever preoccupied him that other thoughts could not get through".

The travellers slept in Munich, eating acorn coffee, black bread and turnip jam. From then on Young took charge and they travelled on through Berlin, home. Though more than capable of finding his way in the mountains and avoiding danger, Lunn needed a guide for ordinary journeys. He used to say this was the start of his career as a helpee.

He went back to Germany on 29 January with Joris Young, who was there as a War Correspondent for the Daily News. They stayed in Berlin for a few days, struggling with bureaucracy during the day and going to the theatre in the evenings. Lunn talked to other travellers on the trains to get news of deprivation in other towns. He remarked with satisfaction that "of all countries engaged in this war, the English seem to have got a clean record as far as prisoners are concerned. We are naturally more humane than the French or Germans, but four years of war have not improved us." He went on to Holland, where he enjoyed real cakes and real coffee, and then returned to London. He was meeting other authors and making notes about them in his journal. He thought Alec Waugh was: "a famous 47 author who looks like a nice cheerful lad of 19. Waugh is a brilliant journalist, but is in danger of writing himself out. He wrote on athletics for my book. The article did not contain one idea; the style was vapid and nerveless."

Of S.P.B. Mais, he said: "He has a genius for exploiting those from whom he imagines he can extract something profitable. Before he had known me a week he had invited himself and his wife down to Hastings, an invitation which I regretfully declined. Ackerly told me he had treated his home as a hotel. He seems equally prepared to treat my hotels as his home."

A couple of years later he met Randolph Churchill. They had a lively and controversial discussion that lasted until 4.30 am. Lunn gave a rational rather than emotional defence of Christianity. Churchill said "You're a most entertaining person. Why havn't I met you before?" He told Lunn about his relations with his father, whom he adored. Winston, however, disapproved of him very strongly, saying he spent money much too freely, did no work and seldom read.

Immediately the war was over, Arnold Lunn settled back to looking after his father's clients. The family spent the summers in Grindelwald and the winters in Murren. Hugh, writing under the name Hugh Kingsmill, published a book called "The Will to Love" in 1919, but it had bad reviews. Arnold also continued to write a great deal, sitting at a table with Mabel and Peter. In 1920, "Auction Piquet" (a card game for two which he had invented) appeared under the nom de plume Rubicon. "Cross-country Skiing" followed, also "Was Switzerland Pro German?" under the nom de plume Sutton Croft, and "The Bernese Oberland". So card games, ski technique, politics and travel all provided him with useful subjects. One extract shows his mixture of egotism and self-deprecation: "My letters are really my journal. I write them partly to amuse the recipient, partly to keep a record for myself. On looking back over my old journals, I find a good deal of pretentious stuff with which I now disagree, many bad forecasts and many mistaken judgements.

I find myself distinctly interesting and I am doing my best to provide in my old age a series of first-class authorities and documents for the study of the life and mission of Arnold Lunn. To be called "The Evolution of Lunnism from the Original Documents", 50 copies, privately printed, all numbered - one read."

Mabel's father, the Earl of Iddesleigh, was ill so she went to visit him. Lunn was euphoric when she returned: "Mabel has come back to me. Mabel and Peter and there is quite a new colour in life. I have been married now nearly six years and I am more in love than I ever was as a boy. For I was a boy of 21 when I first met Mabel, and it only took me three days to realise that I had stumbled onto something quite unusually good, though it took me four years to persuade her that my modest request was worthy of prompt attention. She is now 30, but she does not look a day older than when I first met her. I feel quite a lot older and there is a sort of paternal touch about my feelings for this delicate, small, fairylike little person. As she has an equally maternal feeling towards the untidy helpless ass that she has married and that she now manages with such consummate ease, my own relations to myself must be grandparental.

God must have been very pleased when he made her. I suppose there wasn't enough of the very finest material to make her very big, but 4ft 9in of perfect womanhood is worth much more than 5ft 6in of any other possible combination. I really have had astounding luck. Domine non sum dignus." (Lord I am not worthy).

The Federal Council of British Ski Clubs, founded in March 1914 but unable to develop during the war, was reconstituted in 1920. It united the Davos English Ski Club (given precedence as the oldest club), the Ski Club of Great Britain, the Scottish Ski Club, the North of England Ski Club, the British Ski Association and the National Ski Union.

Lunn's work in Murren with the interned, taking tests and conducting a lively correspondence with Vivian Caulfeild on technique, proved invaluable to the new Council. He continued to take second- and third-class tests regularly, helped by Mark Pery (later Earl of Limerick) and Caulfeild. Mabel was at the peak of her skiing career and it was in the 1921-2 season that she passed the SCGB's first-class test.

By the 1920's he was suggesting the use of the Stem-Christiania and admitting that, as he then had an injured right leg on which he had to use a spring binding, he tended to continue to Telemark to the left, but found the Stem-Christiania easier to the right. Hannes Schneider, the great Austrian innovator, who was to become a friend and ally of Lunn, taught that the Stem was easier to control on steep slopes than the Telemark. When Lunn went to visit him in St Anton in 1927, it was largely because Schneider had analysed the Stem turn combined with the Arlberg Crouch, and demonstrated their efficiency.

Meanwhile Lunn was experimenting with different kinds of races. In January 1920 he arranged for competitors to be taken on a tour and marks were given for speed, steadiness and control. A cup – the Alpine Ski Challenge Cup – was awarded to the best runner and was won that year by Mark Pery.

Arnold and Mabel's second son was born on 29 July 1920, but it was not an easy birth. Lunn played chess to try and take his mind off what was happening: "Then suddenly I heard a glorious sound, the cry of the newly arrived John Tristram Northcote Lunn. I went along to Peter's room and woke nanny. Peter sat up. You've got a little brother, I said. "Horst du das, Nanny", said Peter, "Ich ha' ein kleen bruderli". John is an adorable child. I had no idea how he would tug at one's heart. He is not strong and we are worried about him, but he must pull through. The doctor thought he would born dead, but sister persisted that he was alive and she was right."

Wanting a nanny in Switzerland, Lunn went to the Bernese pastor and said he was looking for a good ski-runner who spoke Bernese German. "And character?" asked the pastor. But Arnold said that whereas nurses of good character were common, nurses who could master the Telemark and Bernese dialect were rare. Eventually he engaged the best lady skier in Grindelwald. No wonder his son Peter turned out to be a ski racer!

In 1920, as well as writing books, he took on the joint Editorship, with H. Marriott, of "The British Ski Year Book", published by the Federal Council of British Ski Clubs, of which he was Chairman. The main purposes of the annual were to disseminate useful information on ski tours completed by members, to recommend equipment, and to cover the news of all the clubs belonging to the Federal Council. The Alpine Ski Club Annual was incorporated into the Yearbook of the SCGB from then on.

Marriott retired after three issues, but for more than fifty years Lunn was to continue as Editor. As well as fulfilling all its main aims, he used the publication to fight and win his great battle for downhill ski-racing. As the rules for downhill and slalom were refined, they were published in the Year Book. There were also reports on the classic races that Lunn and his friends, Hannes Schneider, Walter Amstutz and Ernst Gertsch, founded and organised.

The British Ski Year Book remains today an invaluable historical document, as well as an insight into half a century of skiing. Touring information, equipment and news were covered, as was Gerald Seligman's classic research on the structure of the snow crystal and its influence on avalanches. Skiing technique from Telemark to Parallel Swing was documented as it developed. But above all, the Year Book records the development of downhill and slalom racing.

The annual was printed by King & Hutchings of Uxbridge, and Lunn formed an excellent working relationship with a Director of the company, James Hutchings. He was also helped by Colonel Bowdler, who read the proofs. Always careless with papers himself, Lunn often recorded his gratitude for the coordination and corrections that they did for him. The print order for the 1920 edition was 1,500 copies, to be distributed as follows: National Ski Union 168, British Ski Association 301, Ski Club of Great Britain 253, North East Ski Club 33, and Alpine Ski Club 197. Further copies were sold and given to advertisers and contributors.

From the first edition, the BSYB shows the facility with which Arnold Lunn wrote and the humour which he was able to introduce into a scholarly and scientific guide. He was the ideal Editor for, as well as being a lucid writer, passionate skier and ski tourer, the days he had spent trying out turns with Vivian Caulfeild made him a great exponent of ski technique. He tried to persuade Caulfeild that Lifted Stems (which his broken right leg forced him to use himself) were tighter and therefore more effective than the Telemark.

A few weeks after the Armistice, Lunn had written to all the German Honorary Members of the Alpine Ski Club, saying that their names would remain on the Club's list. He hoped that the love of mountains, which they shared, would prove stronger than the differences that had divided them.

In the first issue of the British Ski Year Book, he gave news of W.R. Rickmers, Henry Hoek and Mathias Zdarsky. The first, as a German, had had to work for the General Staff in Berlin, but said he always kicked against being employed in anything directed against England. He was even more in revolt when he had to join the Army as a Private and forfeited any hope of advancement because he refused to 'lick the boots of my superiors'. After the war he joined a publishing firm concerned with alpine publications.

Dr. Henry Hoek, who had co-authored "The Ski-Runner" in 1906 with E.C. Richardson, had escaped twice from plane accidents, in each of which the pilot was killed. Mathias Zdarsky had served as a ski instructor in the Austrian Army and been terribly injured in an avalanche, suffering about eighty fractures and dislocations, including six spinal dislocations.

Lunn wrote "Alpine Skiing at all Heights and Seasons", which was published by Methuen in 1921. This neat booklet, a sequel to "Cross-country Skiing", was easy to fit into a knapsack and covered every aspect of the sport, from getting fit to snowcraft and choosing a route. A mine of useful experience was handed on about how to: turn on a bank rather than in a hollow, avoid trees in warm weather (because melted snow falls off branches), find powder on north-facing slopes, and spring snow on south-facing ones. Wet and dry snow avalanches were analysed. The use of sticks is clearly set out – as a brake they can be helpful, but more often they detract from safety and speed.

The British Ski Championship meeting in Wengen on 5-12 January 1921, organised by Lunn, was the first national championships in the World to include Alpine races. It was to be 1932 before Australia, New Zealand and Germany followed suit, and 1933 for Austria and Switzerland.

The rules for slalom racing were still being defined, so the 1921 British Championships were decided on the combined marking of a downhill race and a style competition. The downhill (known then as the cross-country championship) started about 152m below the Lauberhorn and finished on a little shelf below the Salzegg just beside Buss Bridge, which gave a descent of about 488m. Dangerous rocks were marked by flags. In the style competition, competitors were required to make four linked Telemarks, Stemming Turns and Jump Turns, and also two series of four stop Christianias each way. However, the points were weighted in favour of speed in the downhill, for "though control is important, dash and speed are more important".

The race was won by Leonard Dobbs, whose brother Bill and sister Kitty were also ski racers. Their father, George Dobbs, had been a Director of Henry Lunn's tourist agency, and the children had been brought up to ski. Kitty, who became British Lady Ski Champion in 1924, later married Malcolm Muggeridge, and was responsible for a lasting friendship between Arnold Lunn and Muggeridge, which was fostered as much by discussion of religion as by skiing.

Lunn was not satisfied with the rules for the slalom as run in the first British Championships. He felt that style marks were unnecessary. The slalom had originated in Norway as a steep run through trees, which forced skiers to turn. Zdarsky, at the turn of the century, had organised a descent of some 750m on a heavily controlled course, which he called "a slalom". It was a test of mountain skiing, but was not a race. Style was more important than speed and everyone who covered the course within a fixed time received a prize. Competitors carried rucksacks and there was no restriction on stick-riding. Fritz Huitfeld, in a book on skiing published in 1908, described a Norwegian slalom: "For such a track no kind of preparations were made. Everything remained as in nature".

Zdarsky had been the first to produce an intelligible analysis of a Stemming Turn and the first to start a school to teach the art of skiing on steep Alpine ground. Lunn gave him the credit for being the father of Alpine skiing. Then Hannes Schneider had developed the Arlberg Crouch and taught it successfully in his school. Lunn was to take the development a step further.

On 1 April 1921 Arnold Lunn was nominated President of the Federal Council of British Ski Clubs, the top job in skiing at that time. Even so he was still not acceptable to the Alpine Club. Captain Farrer, the then recently retired President, wrote to him on 4 December 1921: "The objection to you entering the Club is that the membership might possibly be used by you or your company as a kind of advertisement. I am quite willing to believe that you would not yourself do this, but it would be very difficult to bind a company". Lunn wrote back refuting this, but to no avail. In fact his Application Form, which is still held by the Alpine Club, shows that the Committee would have accepted him because of his mountaineering record. But the unseen hands of members had blackballed him.

He made a formal application in 1922 with Martin Conway as Proposer and Farrar as Seconder. Winthrop Young, Schester and Reade were cited as supporters, but the application failed at the ballot at the General Meeting. It was a blow.

In the 1922 British Ski Year Book, Lunn defined the slalom as a race over steep and difficult ground to test turns. In the race he organised that year for the Anglo-Swiss Universities, he placed flags in pairs down a slope to force the racer to make difficult turns. The race simulated speed through a wood – trees provide natural obstacles. It was not practical for racers to be guided round trees, so poles with flags were substituted. In Zdarsky's slaloms, competitors turned round single poles and were marked for style. Lunn's slaloms tested speed and pairs of flags forced competitors to turn where it was difficult to do so. Lunn was against marking for style as a fast ugly turn was better than a slow pretty one. Time penalties were given for a fall (10 seconds), for a hand touching the snow (5 seconds), and for touching the control flags.

Walter Amstutz, writing years later in the "Schneehase", the Swiss Academic Skiclub Annual, described how Zdarsky's slalom varied from Lunn's. "The characteristic of a race is wholly missing, for ski-racing was a sport in which Zdarsky never exhibited any real interest. Zdarsky's slalom was judged on style, not speed."

For some years the first run of a slalom was held on hard snow, beaten by the racers, the second on soft snow to simulate skiing offpiste. Racers started in the afternoon in the order in which they had finished in the morning.

On 21 January 1922 the Alpine Ski Challenge Cup was presented for a slalom race, judged on speed alone. Lunn set this – now considered to be the first modern slalom – on the practice slopes at Murren. It was won by J.A. Joannides, R.B. McConnell was second and Dame Katharine Furse third. In 1922 "Style Competitions and Slalom Races" was printed and the rules also appeared in the Public Schools Alpine Ski Club Year Book dated 1923. This race became an integral part of the British Ski Championships on 2 January 1926 in Gstaad, when it was won by Bill Dobbs.

The Alpine Ski Club and the British Ski Association both bought copies of Lunn's "Guide to the Bernese Oberland" for all their members.

In 1923 the British Championships meeting was held in Murren, but Lunn was ill. A bad cold had led to a mastoid operation, so he was unable to set the championship courses. Alan d'Egville, a regular Murren visitor and part of the inner circle of friends, set the courses and wrote the report for the British Ski Year Book. Some used the Telemark, others the Stem turn. Hugh Dowding, then an SCGB rep and later to be a famous military leader, won, followed by T.F. Barratt, J.A. Joannides, L. Dobbs and Howard Ford. Ford was only 15 at the time – a promising newcomer.

Meanwhile, with his friends, Lunn explored the mountains and published his experiences in the British Ski Year Book. True to his attitude to lady skiers, and influenced perhaps by Mabel's courage and skill as a skier, Lunn suggested in 1923 that it was time a ski club was formed especially for ladies. Mabel, Doreen Elliott, Mrs Duncan Harvey and others held the first meeting of the Ladies Ski Club in Murren in January. Lunn, ineligible for membership of course, was presented with a badge that carried the bar sinister – his official title was 'Sinister Father of the Club', and as such he was always invited to their celebrations.

Years later he was to write that he had enticed some prominent lady ski-runners into Room 4 of the Palace Hotel, which he used as his office. He read to them the rules that he had drafted and told them they were founder members. They viewed his suggestion with dark suspicion, for it was thought to be a sop, as membership of the Alpine Ski Club was at that time closed to ladies. He insisted that his only hope was that the first ladies' ski club in the World would be formed by the British. In fact there had been ladies' ski clubs organised in Scandinavia many years before. The Ladies' Ski Club was to thrive and to this day organises very successful races each year. In 1929 the Swiss girls formed their own club, the Schweizerische Damen Skiklub, to race against the British girls, but it closed down after nearly half a century.

The appeal of skiing was growing and the Federal Council was active. Over 200 members attended the Council's Dinner at the Trocadero on 22 March 1923. The British Ski Championship meeting was held in Adelboden from 3 January 1924. Lunn then went to Murren until the end of February, and then on to Chalet Berna in Grindelwald, always working for his father.

Ladies races continued and the first Lady Denman Challenge Cup was held from the Schiltgrat in Murren in January 1924. The entry list included a name unfamiliar to Lunn – Martha Mainwaring. In those days all racers started together, in what was known as a geschmozzle start.

Years later Lunn described what happened. "Betty Schuster was leading comfortably when suddenly from behind a rock a dreadful apparition appeared – a rouged and powdered female in wig, jumper and skirt. Suddenly I realised that Martha was none other than Antony, Viscount Knebworth. He set off in hot pursuit of Betty Schuster, who was put off by this unknown female and lost the race. I skied down to the finish, furious with Antony for ragging an important race. 'Don't you recognise this jumper?', asked Antony. 'No, why the hell should I?', I replied. 'Only because it's Mabel's'."

Knebworth, in a letter from Murren to his mother, wrote that he had told Lunn in advance about the joke and been warned against it, but Mabel had persuaded him to go ahead.

The Kandahar Ski Club was founded on 30 January 1924, in Room 4 of the old wing of the Palace Hotel in Murren, which was later burnt down. The aim was to raise the standard of downhill and slalom racing and to secure international recognition for those events. Anthony Angas was appointed the first President, Duncan Harvey the Honorary Secretary. Mabel, Mrs Harvey, Dora Fox, Captain Strickland, T.F. Barratt, Alan d'Egville and Geoffrey Samuelson were all present. There is no doubt that Arnold Lunn was the moving spirit. Bedford Russell F.R.C.S., who was not there, was elected Vice-President.

Among the founder members were Adrian Allinson, the artist, and Andrew Irvine, who disappeared on Everest with Mallory later in the year. Young Peter Lunn, aged 9, was upstairs in bed, but next morning his father told him he had been elected a member of this new club.

The club was named after the race - by then well-established - the Roberts of Kandahar. Various suggestions were made for a badge, but Alan d'Egville was adamant that it should be a simple K. "If they ask you what it means", he said, "tell them you can bloody well find out for yourself".

Another landmark in the history of skiing that year was the foundation of the International Ski Federation. A Commission had been in existence since 1909 and the first International Ski Congress was held in Kristiania (later renamed Oslo) in 1910. Austria, Bohemia, England, France, Germany, Norway, Scotland, Spain, Sweden and Switzerland were all represented. The Commission was charged with working out statutes and rules. In keeping with the fact that ski racing was primarily Nordic in those days, the first Commission consisted of two Norwegians and a Swede.

Congresses were held regularly but, largely because of the disruption of World War I, the International Ski Federation was not officially founded until 2 February 1924, during an international winter sports week in Chamonix. This was later recognised as the first Winter Olympic Games.

Even then, the influence was largely Scandinavian - the first President was Colonel Holmquist of Sweden and the Vice-President was Major Oestgaard of Norway.

The only skiing events at the Chamonix Games were langlauf and ski-jumping. The founder members of the International Ski Federation (FIS) were Austria, Czechoslovakia, Finland, France, Great Britain, Hungary, Italy, Yugoslavia, Norway, Poland, Romania, Sweden, Switzerland and the USA.

Although Lunn thoroughly approved of the Federal Council joining the FIS, he did suggest that care should be taken that the British contribution towards the expenses of the new organisation would be limited. He said the various countries' contributions should be based on their memberships. At one time it had been suggested that each country should contribute £100 but this, he pointed out, would mean each British skier giving two shillings, whereas each German would only be giving the equivalent of a penny a head.

In the same month, Lunn organised the first international event to be decided on the Alpine combination of downhill and slalom. The downhill was run down Tschuggen Glade in Wengen, and was won by A. Gertsch, who beat Christopher Mackintosh by 5 seconds and went on to win the combined. Peter Lunn, aged 9, competed and beat a Swiss and a Briton. This race was the forerunner of the Anglo-Swiss team races.

It was also in 1924 that Lunn was told by a distinguished surgeon that if he continued to walk on his injured leg without support, he would be a cripple in ten years and that a bad skiing fall would have very serious consequences. "Acting on his advice, I had my leg fitted with a steel contraption of great weight and became an Honorary Lady for whose benefit young girls rose sympathetically in crowded buses and offered the poor cripple a seat.

I might still be wearing this contraption, which did not make skiing any easier, had not the British Universities defeated the Swiss Universities in January 1925. At the Dinner which followed this happy event, the steel contraption somehow went through a plate glass window and spent the night in the snow. I had some difficulty in readjusting to it when it was returned next morning by the concierge and I discarded it a few days later. Having resigned from the Honorary Ladies Club, I won the Scaramanga Cup for roped ski-racing, partnered by Adrian Allinson, and a few weeks later made a new ski route up the Eiger, in the course of which I was on my legs from ten at night until four the following afternoon".

Lunn had finished "Roman Converts", which was published in 1924. Still intensely interested in religion, he wrote it to refute Knox's arguments in favour of Catholicism. Also published that year was "Skiing for Beginners".

Lunn's friendship with Walter Amstutz had grown with the years. Amstutz had done well at school and went on to university. Amstutz and Willy Richardet were students at Bern University – Lunn described them as brilliant and daring mountaineers and first-class ski-runners. In the intervals between skiing, Amstutz studied economics, eventually gaining a doctorate. He spent a term at London University, where Lunn said: "He acquired an insight into that branch of economics which deals with the comparative rate at which money disappears in London and in Bern. His researches were so interesting that his family recalled him to Switzerland".

Lunn arranged to meet Willy Richardet in Grindelwald on the evening of 16 May 1924 to make the first ski ascent of the Eiger. In the late afternoon of 17 May, Lunn was watching from the Eigerjoch station. Amstutz and Richardet were exploring the Eiger glacier, by which on the following day they were all to approach the summit. Suddenly a great sheet of ice peeled off the cliffs of the Monch and thundered down onto the slopes that Amstutz and Richardet were exploring. "Poor devils", said a guide, "they'll be killed for sure". Had the two men been unroped their chances of escape would have been greater. As it was, their race to escape the avalanche was not only infinitely the most exciting race Lunn ever watched, but also the most impressive. They kept their nerve and the proper intervals between them, avoided tripping over the rope or being jerked off their feet. To Lunn's unutterable relief and gratitude, the avalanche missed them.

Lunn, Amstutz, Richardet and Fritz Amacher achieved the first ski ascent of the Eiger by the Eigerjoch. Amacher, who was liftman at the Baer Hotel in Grindelwald, carried Lunn's skis. Lunn wrote of him: "He seems to find the gentle exercise of starting the lift all the training he requires before setting off to carry two pairs of ski up several thousand feet." In the 1965 British Ski Year Book he wrote: "Fritz Amacher was a wonderful weight carrier…but for his help my game leg would have prevented me from tackling those exceptionally long days. I was very fond of Fritz and enjoyed his pawky sense of humour. He was attacked by guides for acting as my porter on our ski ascent of the Eiger, for theoretically a porter is not allowed to accompany a guideless climber above the snowline. He replied: "If I choose to climb the Eiger with my old friend Lunn, what the devil has that got to do with you?"

Even without carrying his skis, Lunn took on a tremendous physical feat. They left the Eiger glacier station at 10.25pm and climbed steadily through the moonlight for about four hours, climbed the ice wall and crossed two crevasses. It was an extremely dangerous route. At one point Lunn failed to clear his crampons of snow, slipped and went hurtling down the slope. He said he felt no fear, only a petulant irritation with himself. Amstutz, who was roped to him, also hurtled down to what seemed certain disaster, as the ice slope curved over to a glacier 500ft below. Fortunately a small spike of rock, three inches broad and an inch in height, held the rope, soft snow prevented it being cut and they came to a stop.

Timing played an important part in that expedition. Lunn had noticed that the damp wet snow of May often slid off the buttress of the Monch onto the glacier at the precise moment when the evening Sun left the slope, the sudden change of temperature producing this effect. So they left the Scheidegg nearly two hours before midnight; none too early as it happened, for an hour after they returned the expected avalanche swept down the slope on which they had been skiing. Walter Amstutz wrote years later that descending was a far more fatiguing matter, particularly for Arnold, who complained bitterly about an atrocious pain in his right leg. It was while resting on the Eigerjoch during this expedition that Amstutz told

Lunn he proposed to found a Swiss University Ski Club to campaign with the British for the recognition of Alpine racing and to compete with them in team races. The Schweizerische Academische Ski-Klub (SAS) was duly founded in Bern in November and the international races that started in January were run as the Anglo-Swiss University Races. When the battle hotted up for recognition of downhill and slalom, the SAS, with Amstutz as its mouthpiece, solidly backed their introduction.

6

1925-28 Hannes Schneider, Arlberg-Kandahar & Inferno

By spending the winters in Murren, Lunn had made it a financial success for his father's company. It was considered the smart place to visit. The Public Schools Alpine Sports Club had brought the Lunns many rich, influential and aristocratic friends. The Kandahar Ski Club formed the nucleus and attracted other international figures. Lady Mabel was the perfect hostess at the big round table at the entrance to the Palace Hotel dining room, and the social life at night was as important as the sporting life by day.

Hugh Dowding (later to become Air Chief Marshal), Antony Knebworth (heir to Lord Lytton) and E.C. Pery (later Earl of Limerick) were all part of the inner circle, together with the Dobbs, "Johan" Joannides, Alan d'Egville (who provided a lot of humour) and, of course, expert racers such as Chris Mackintosh, Bill Bracken and Walter Amstutz. The British lady racers, including Esme Mackinnon, Doreen Elliott, Audrey Sale Barker and Katharine Furse, were the best in the World.

Meanwhile, the British ski establishment was sorting itself out. In the autumn of 1924 four wise men - Alex Keiller and Gerald Seligman of the Ski Club of Great Britain and E.C. Pery and Arnold Lunn representing the British Ski Association - came to an agreement. In return for the SCGB dropping its qualification for membership – so that it would accept novices – the British Ski Association agreed to the Ski Club of Great Britain's name being used for a new national club. A final draft of the new Constitution was sent to SCGB members in April 1925 and a meeting was held on 7 July. From then on, the Federal Council was dissolved and the SCGB took over. The Alpine Ski Club and the SCGB shared the British Ski Year Book, which Lunn continued to edit.

Lunn was at the Palace Hotel in Murren until the end of February 1925, then in March he took a holiday. The first half of April was spent at The Albany in Hastings, looking after his father's business there and he then went to Chalet Berna in Grindelwald.

The British Ski Championship meeting in 1925 was scheduled for Pontresina, but had to be cancelled due to lack of snow. The Anglo-Swiss University Races were held on Scheidegg. The downhill was full of excitement because Walter Amstutz and Christopher Mackintosh (an amazing athlete and British record holder in several sports, including the long jump) were keen rivals. Mackintosh made a flying start but suffered a series of disasters, falling into a stream, colliding with a tree and dropping a sheer 20ft into another stream. No wonder then that Amstutz, described by Lunn as a brilliant ski-runner, won. Antony Knebworth upheld British pride by coming second and, despite all his problems, Mackintosh came in third.

The slalom runs were held across the valley in Murren, the first on hard snow, the second on soft and on combined results the Swiss won, Amstutz taking first place, Mackintosh second and Knebworth third. At this time both the Telemark and Christiania were used for downhill racing. Mackintosh, who took practically everything straight anyway, used the Telemark. Amstutz, with sounder judgement as to whether he could go straight or not, crouched with skis together on steep slopes. Leonard Dobbs, though not as strong as Mackintosh, had a flair for ski country and good judgement. He used the Telemark on soft snow and also ran straight in the Telemark position.

In 1925 a daughter, Jaqueta, was born to join Peter and John. That year also, "The Mountains of Youth" was published by Eyre and Spottiswood. This was an account of Lunn's climbing and ski-touring experiences since he was a boy. He told of his accident at Cyfrwy and his more recent exploits with Amstutz and Richardet. Lunn was in London in October and November, then went to the Palace Hotel in Murren until 7 March, then back to London until the beginning of May, when he went to Grindelwald.

On 17 May 1925 Prince Chichibu of Japan came to spend a few days with Arnold and Mabel Lunn at their chalet in Grindelwald. Lunn took him ski touring with Adolf Rubi and Fritz Steuri as their principal guides. Max Amstutz, Walter's brother, took a cine film of the tour. On the 18th they left for the Jungfraujoch, on the 20th they climbed the Wannehorn, and the next day made the first ski traverse of the Bieliegerlucke from the Finsteraarhorn Hut to the Rhone Valley. An attempt on Mont Leone was ruined by bad weather, so they returned to the Bernese Oberland, where they made the first ski ascent of the Grindelwald Grunhorn.

In 1926 the British Ski Championship meeting was to be held in Gstaad starting on 2 January. The slalom was again on soft and hard snow (though hard snow was difficult to find at the time). As the snow conditions were so bad and most competitors came from the Oberland, it was agreed by all that they should go back to Wengen and run the downhill there. It was held on 4 January from the Lauberhorn and Christopher Mackintosh won easily. In a Novices Race for those who had only skied one season, young Jimmy Riddell showed early promise in beating 32 others to win. He was to be an important character in British skiing for the next 75 years.

The SAS, led by Walter Amstutz, organised the first International University downhill and slalom race in St Moritz, with Austrian, British, German, Italian and Swiss competitors. M. de Mestral, Tourist Office Director of St Moritz, wanted to set an old style slalom himself around single flags. This, said Walter Amstutz, was the only time he saw Lunn "boiling mad" and insisting on setting the slalom himself. In 1926 the Ski Club of Great Britain, prompted by Lunn, circulated to every national skiing organisation an appeal for comments and official recognition of downhill and slalom racing. Not one reply was received.

Lunn wrote an article on the same lines for the British Ski Year Book. He also claimed that langlauf was bad for the heart. But, always fair, in the same issue he printed a defence of langlauf written by Count Hamilton, Honorary Secretary of the FIS. It shows how well the two men understood the problems. F.S. Smythe, the mountaineer and author, was another contributor to the Year Book.

Downhill and slalom were discussed at a FIS Committee Meeting in Cortina early in 1927, but a decision was postponed until the International Ski Congress in St Moritz in February 1928, where a special committee was set up to discuss the problems.

Before then, Lunn had reached another landmark in his life. In 1927 he went with Alan d'Egville, contributor of many witty articles to the Year Book, to spend a weekend in Kitzbuhel with Major R.J. Bracken, father of ski racer Bill Bracken. Unexpectedly, an entertaining Canadian, Bill Adamson, appeared in Kitzbuhel with instructions to bring Lunn and Bracken to St Anton-am-Arlberg – if necessary by force! Walter Bernays, an American who had skied all over the World and, as Lunn reported, done some pioneering work in the Rockies, had been reading the British Ski Year Books. He was determined to convince Lunn that the Stem and Arlberg Crouch taught by Hannes Schneider were the best way to ski.

Two years younger than Arnold Lunn, Schneider had begun to ski when 8 on barrel staves in the Arlberg, and had his first pair of skis in 1903. As he grew up he found the Telemark (developed on gentle Scandinavian slopes) difficult on the steep Austrian slopes, and so he changed to the Stem-Christie. In 1920 a Dr Arnold Fanck began work on a film called "Der Wunder des Schneeschuhs", which was to become a classic. Fanck had met the young Schneider skiing in Davos in 1912 and filmed him to demonstrate technique. By that time Schneider was also well known as a competitor, including ski jumping and the early form of style slalom. He ran the Arlberg Skischool, where he taught the Stem and the Crouch. He was also tall, well-built and very good-looking, with a captivating smile. The films made him internationally famous.

Well aware of Schneider's reputation and encouraged by the possibility of a good argument about technique, Arnold Lunn and Alan d'Egville stopped off at St Anton on their return journey from Kitzbuhel. Immediately Lunn and Schneider formed a mutual respect and friendship. Lunn described Schneider as a magnetic personality with a genius for leadership.

They had useful discussions and, on the afternoon before he left St Anton, Lunn bought a small cup. With the help of Walter Bernays, he set a slalom on the nursery slopes for the boys of the village. This was the first modern slalom set in Austria. The boys were delighted with what was, to them, an unknown type of race. Before leaving, Lunn and Schneider planned that a cup, to be called the Arlberg-Kandahar, should be presented by the Kandahar for a combined downhill and slalom event the following year in the Arlberg. This was a year before the FIS had given even provisional recognition to the British rules for downhill and slalom.

Lunn was used to encouraging boys to race. In Murren at that time he used to take any youngsters who enjoyed skiing up the mountain and set them off to race back to the village. Marc Hodler, later to take part in many Anglo-Swiss races and to be President of the FIS from 1951-98, remembered those races. "One of the first times we had a race with a geschmozzle start on the Schiltgrat. We had to climb – there were no skilifts then. There were big explanations and I had no idea what to do, you had to go to certain points, not take short cuts. I was very bad in English, but Peter helped me." That was in 1926, when Marc Hodler was 8 and Peter Lunn was 11. So Lunn knew the St Anton boys would be enthusiastic about his new race.

As well as writing and working for his father, Lunn gave talks. In 1927 he was elected Vice-President of the Ski Club of Great Britain. On 29

November that year he gave a lecture at the Hyde Park Hotel, illustrated by a cinematograph film on skiing. More than 500 members and their friends came to listen. "A History of Skiing" and "Things that have Puzzled Me" were published. He edited the Year Book mainly from Switzerland.

It was in 1928 that the Inferno Race, off-piste from the Schilthorn above Murren to Lauterbrunnen, was first run. It was planned by Lunn, Harold Mitchell, Antony Knebworth, Pelham Maitland, Patsy Richardson and Bunny Ford, all members of the Kandahar. Patsy Richardson could not race as he had sprained an ankle, so he and Lunn synchronised their watches and he went down to Lauterbrunnen to await the racers' arrival. Harold Mitchell won, completing the long course in 1 hour 12 minutes. Doreen Elliott, despite losing nearly ten minutes climbing back to help a competitor who had broken a rib, came fourth and Lunn himself, complete with starter's watch, came sixth equal with d'Egville.

In February 1928 the second Winter Olympic Games were held in St Moritz. The events included a military patrol race, a 50km race and an 18km race, the main jumping competition, and a combined event consisting of cross-country and jumping. Not long before the Congress held during the Games, Count Hamilton visited Murren with his wife, to get first-hand experience of the British innovations.

At the Congress, the Norwegians proposed Lunn's election to the committee and Alex Keiller represented the Ski Club of Great Britain, as an advisor. Herr von Graffenried in the Chair opened with a speech in which he said the Swiss had tried the slalom and been dissatisfied with it - but this had been the old type of slalom with single flags. On the whole, the Scandinavians considered that both downhill running and turning were well tested in langlauf races and the new proposals were artificial. They were suitable only for those who skied for short holidays and were neither strong enough nor experienced enough to compete in langlauf events. It was even suggested that downhill racing was being promoted by British hoteliers as their clients did not have time during their holidays to get fit enough for cross-country.

Lunn countered that langlauf in no way tested downhill racing. He used the analogy of a Cresta tobogganer being forced to run along the flat before and after completing the Cresta course. The downhill should stand on its own. Dr Carl Roesen, the German representative, supported the British proposal. He said the Anglo-Swiss University Races at St Moritz in 1926, when Lunn had set the slalom, had converted him. Another convert was the Swedish representative Carl Nordenson, who edited the Swedish Ski Year Book. Count Hamilton had contributed an article to this book, which convinced Nordenson that the British proposal should be taken seriously. Dr Danegger of Switzerland also supported the British proposals.

Austria was not represented on the Committee; the Swiss were lukewarm in Britain's favour; the Norwegian said he did not like the British rules because they forbade stick riding; the Czech said their programmes were so overcrowded they couldn't find space for downhill. Had it not been for Count Hamilton and Dr Roesen, Lunn's proposal would not have had a chance.

Finally it was decided, backed by Count Hamilton, that associations represented on the FIS should try out the British rules during the next two years and report their conclusions to the Congress at Oslo in 1930. Nicolai Oestgaard of the FIS asked Lunn what he would say if the Norwegians tried to reform the rules of cricket. The reply was: "I wish they would. We might have fewer draws." At the same Congress the question of ladies' races was discussed and Lunn was dismayed that the ladies were considered something of a joke. He recalled that in the Inferno that year Doreen Elliott had done so well.

The first Arlberg-Kandahar was held at the end of March 1928 and is the World's senior international challenge cup decided on downhill and slalom which is open to all comers. Its only predecessors were the British Ski Championships and the Anglo-Swiss University races, both of which of course had restricted entries.

Sadly, Lunn was prevented 'owing to private reasons' (work for his father perhaps) from attending. So Alan d'Egville was in charge of the group that left Murren to compete. The competitors raced not for their countries, but for their clubs. The Kandahar party, which included Charles Proctor of the American Olympic team, met Walter Amstutz and members of the Swiss University Ski Club at Zurich, from where all went on to St Anton by rail.

The invaluable Walter Bernays played a part in the organisation, as did Dr Gomperz, President of the Arlberg Ski School. But it was Hannes Schneider who was the driving force. Unable to race himself because of an injury (his brother Friedrich won the downhill), he had gathered an entry of 45 racers from all over Germany and Austria to compete with the British, Swiss and Americans in the Kandahar group.

He explained the rules of the slalom, assisted the starter, and his instruction had obviously influenced the racers' technique. Alan d'Egville noticed that the Telemark was hardly used. Those who were most successful used Schneider's Arlberg Crouch. Jump turns, up on two sticks, were used by some competitors, but d'Egville reported that they were not as successful as single-stick turns.

Frau Poland, from Vienna, won the ladies combined, with Doreen Elliott winner of the slalom and second overall. The men's cup was won by Benno Laubner from Innsbruck, much to the anger of the Arlbergers who, by adding the times rather than the points of the slalom and downhill, had calculated that Friedrich Schneider had won. D'Egville typically made a joke of the English and Austrian calculations and insisted that his drinks bill according to the English reckoning was five rather than twenty Austrian schillings. The party after the race, with the infectious jollity of d'Egville and the warm hospitality of Schneider, set a tradition for future A-K meetings.

Lunn was to write in "Come What May", published in 1940, "If I am remembered at all after I die, I shall be remembered not as a writer, but as the founder of the Arlberg-Kandahar and as the inventor of the slalom race, both of which will, I believe, survive for many years and perhaps for many centuries." Until Serge Lang founded the World Cup in 1967, the

Arlberg-Kandahar was the most important race of the season – and one with a great atmosphere.

In May 1928 Lunn, with Josef Knubel, toured up the Lauteraar Glacier for six hours and wrote some glowing prose: "Only the rose of dawn and the blue of the sky relieved the monotony of black and white, for winter is never so visibly queen of the High Alps as in the month that witnesses her passing. Suddenly Knubel's axe carved a breach in the cornice that crowned our pass. I scrambled through the gap and looked down on Grindelwald in her habit of spring. It is contrast, and contrast only which reveals the miracle of May. In the valley the slow approach of spring dulls the surprise of her beauty and the mountaineer who spends long days among the glaciers and then suddenly reaches a window from which he can look down on to the valleys feels as if he had never begun to appreciate the colouring of May. Certainly on the Lauteraarsattel I felt that I had never really seen this new and glorious green, a green with a suggestion of the transparent as if I were looking at a view painted on stained glass through which the Sun was shining. The effect was intensified by the contrast with the snowy expanse in our immediate foreground. If I had been dropped by helicopter or reached it by ski lift, the effect of that unique view would have been incomparably less impressive."

Lunn's "Switzerland" was published in 1928, covering the country's history, geography, legends, government and literature. He had undertaken a great deal of research into the works of poets such as Ruskin, Wordsworth and Byron, artists such as Segantini, and writers like Voltaire, Rousseau and de Saussure.

7

1929-35 Catholicism - and Downhill - Accepted

THE 1928-9 SEASON started with perfect weather for ski-racing in Switzerland. There was 3ft of snow in the Engadine and the higher parts of the Oberland. A general thaw on 28 December, and rain below 1,300m, just settled the snow on the upper slopes and from the 31st it was cloudy and cold for a week then clear. There was Sun and frost until the 15th so the slalom for the British Ski Championships was run on good hard snow on the morning of 13th January and powder in the afternoon. Light snow was then followed by heavy falls, from the 17th until the 21st.

Early in 1929 the Polish Ski Association organised European Ski Championships at Zakopane and included a downhill. Lunn did not go himself because the family firm was suffering from the recession. He could not pay his way and would not ask the SCGB to pay his expenses as manager so, although there would have been no downhill race but for him, he was not there to see it.

The official ladies race was a six-kilometre langlauf, so Lunn wrote a carefully worded letter asking if the downhill was open to all amateurs and was told it was. He therefore entered a British team of seven men and two ladies. The Poles then told him that there was no precedent for entering ladies, to which he replied that so far as downhill ski racing was concerned the British created rather than followed precedents. He said afterwards that the Poles very charmingly accepted Doreen Elliott and Audrey Sale-Barker.

They achieved splendid results, coming 13th and 14th and beating 45 men. When they entered a restaurant in Warsaw for dinner after the race, everyone stood up and clapped. The British men, too, had distinguished themselves, with Bill Bracken finishing 2nd, Guy Nixon 6th, James Riddell 8th, F.P Maitland 10th, E.W.A. Richardson 12th and C. Pitman 15th. Harold Mitchell, in spite of breaking a ski and covering most of the course on just the remaining one, came 24th.

The 1929 A-K, held again in St Anton, attracted 106 entries, including 22 ladies. Lunn and Schneider worked happily together and Lunn wrote later that no welcome could have been warmer than the royal welcome with which he was greeted by old friends in the Arlberg. Hannes Schneider, Dr. Gomperz and Walter Bernays worked like Trojans. Gomperz, of the Arlberg Ski Club, as well as timing the slalom and working out the logarithm tables for the combined result, presided over the prize giving and made a witty speech. There is no doubt that the success of the A-K led to the slalom being adopted by the FIS in 1930.

In the Roberts of Kandahar, held that year in Murren, about half the competitors fell at Shambles Corner. Lunn reported: "Above the din I heard the voice of Lady Raeburn exhorting the diminutive figure of her son, Digby, not to ski too fast and to let the big people through the gap first, advice which Digby Raeburn blandly ignored."

Raeburn was to play a big part in British skiing, first as a successful racer, then setting courses and helping as a race official. Respected in the world of British ski politics, he finished a distinguished military career as a General and retired as Governor of the Tower of London, proving an excellent host to clubs and visiting foreign skiers.

Greta Raeburn's pride in her son at the age of 12 was mirrored by Arnold Lunn's in Peter, who was two years older. He realised and laughed at himself for it, quoting in 1940 Greta Raeburn saying to Godi Michel, while watching a race: "Hush Godi, that's sacrilege. Even the choughs have stopped squawking, for Peter is just due to start".

The Year Book continued to be filled with useful and extremely readable advice to skiers. The 1929 edition contains a report from Hannes Schneider (translated by ever-helpful Walter Bernays) about an avalanche on the Festkogel, near Obergurgl. A warning was given about skiers failing to keep to the leader's track and cutting a block of snow off above the rest of the party. Accounts of other accidents followed, including the finding of Captain Marden's body on Aconcagua. He had been an enthusiastic skier in Davos, and the Mardens Ski Club was named after him.

Many climbs and tours are described in the Year Book, but it is still ski racing that fills most of the pages. A major article was aimed at the FIS, encouraging them to adopt the British downhill and slalom rules. Lunn rightly argued that those who skied for enjoyment could not always find the correct facilities to jump and did not always want to make long langlauf treks. The thrill of skiing came in Alpine events.

Lunn had the foresight to realise that British results that year were probably as good as they would ever be. In the Review of the Year he wrote: "It will be very difficult for future British teams to better the performance of our team at Zakopane. Competition is bound to become more intense. We are hopelessly outnumbered. Our rivals have 20, 30 or 40 times as many skiers from whom to select a team. We shall be racing men with short holidays against men who are on ski for six months of the year."

The 1930 Roberts of Kandahar, held on 4 January, showed how rugged the conditions were compared with the manicured courses raced over today. Christopher Mackintosh had to crash through bushes to avoid Howard Ford, but still won. Ford hit a fence and went right through it. Young Digby Raeburn skied with great self-possession to come second. Esme Mackinnon won the Ladies Championship straight race (in spite of falling into a ditch) and the slalom, with Nell Carroll second and Di Crewdson third. It was heartening to see how good the teenage racers were.

In the battle for the recognition of the British race rules for downhill and slalom, great progress was made at the FIS Congress held in Oslo in 1930. By now Lunn had many friends in high places and since the 1928 Olympics he had had an opportunity to show the importance of this kind of event. The FIS was still dominated by Scandinavians, with Holmquist of Sweden as President and Oestgaard of Norway as Vice-President. But both men had open minds and had taken the trouble to attend the Anglo-Swiss University Races, where the British Universities beat the Swiss for the second time in succession.

Also Colonel Christian Krefting, a former winner of the Norwegian Ski Championships, wrote an article in the "Aftenposten" newspaper about watching a Roberts of Kandahar race in Murren. He went to the race intending to show what skiing really was, but left in admiration of: "Those plucky young Englishmen coming down those steep hills with incredible speed. To get down in the usual Norwegian way was quite impossible."

On 22 February 1930 Lunn left Murren for Oslo with Pelham Maitland to represent the Ski Club of Great Britain at the FIS Congress. On the way they met Count Aldo Bonacossa, who represented Italy, and Walter Amstutz and Dick Boord joined the party at Basle. Oestgaard was at Oslo Station to welcome them. The Committee set up to study downhill and slalom rules met in Finse. Twenty-one years before, Lunn had returned from this Norwegian village to keep an appointment with Canon Savage at Hexham, where he had met Mabel for the first time. It was a good omen.

In the Year Book he summarised progress so far. In 1921 a downhill race had been included in the British National Championships. In 1926 he had issued a memorandum asking for recognition of the downhill rules. In 1928 at the FIS Congress in St Moritz, it had been agreed that all the nations represented at the Congress should experiment and report to a Committee on Alpine Racing.

As a result, the attitude of the European nations was changing. The Anglo-Swiss University Races had done admirable work for the cause. Dr. Danegger, President of the FIS Rules Committee (and one-time President of the Swiss Ski Association), had originally been against the slalom, but

Walter Amstutz had converted him when he visited Davos during the University Winter Games. In 1929 the Austrian Ski Association sent the Committee a memorandum supporting the recognition of downhill races. The Polish Ski Association had included a downhill at Zakopane. In the summer of 1929, Norway, Sweden and Finland had met and decided to vote for the downhill, though they were still against the slalom.

The Committee to meet in Norway included Count Aldo Bonacossa, Colonel A. Bobkowski of Poland, Karl Danegger, Walter Amstutz, Lieutenant Helset (Vice President of the Norwegian Ski Association) and Lunn. Thanks to careful planning, the help of Amstutz and the fact that Bonacossa and Oestgaard had all seen and realised the potential of Alpine racing, the proposal was, after some tense moments, accepted.

At the Congress, it was agreed that the 1932 Olympics should be held at Lake Placid. The 1931 FIS Championships were to be run by Germany at a resort that did not have a suitable downhill course. Lunn proposed - and it was agreed - that the Ski Club of Great Britain should run the downhill parts of the championships that year in Murren. In his thanks to all those who supported him, Lunn included Fritz Erb of the influential Swiss paper "Sport", who was to prove a good ally for many years. A generation later, his son Karl Erb was also to give good publicity to the Kandahar races in the same paper.

Lunn took the opportunity to do some skiing around Finse - recalling his last visit in 1909 - and he set a slalom which, with Walter Amstutz to demonstrate, proved popular. He wrote afterwards that he could understand the disinterest in slalom among the Norwegians because their slopes were so much less steep than the Alps.

He praised the proverbial hospitality of the Scandinavians and said: "The arch heretic was made to feel thoroughly at home in the Rome of our skiing world". In the 1930 Year Book he included a Norwegian impression of skiing in Murren and an article by Captain Oestgaard.

Bill Bracken became a ski-teacher in 1930 and was made an Honorary Member of the Kandahar, as they could not accept a professional as an ordinary member. Ski-teachers, however, were not classed as professionals under FIS rules. The Kandahar Ski Club was proving so popular that The

Lone Tree Club had been set up in Murren to accommodate many skiers who wanted to join the Kandahar, but were not eligible.

Lunn had been a smoker and had tried to give it up in 1928 without success, but in 1930 he gave it up for good. He also discouraged all Junior K's from taking up smoking.

His book "The Complete Ski-Runner" was published in 1930. In it he explained that he used the words ski-running rather than skiing to describe downhill skiing. The book did not cover ski-jumping, ski-mountaineering or langlauf racing, which he thought the "complete skier" should know about. The book was published by Methuen in a series about sports, which included The Complete Yachtsman, Golfer and Mountaineer.

At the time of the Arlberg-Kandahar that year, Lunn was in Norway and Hannes Schneider in Japan, but it was still a big race. The report, written by Major Bracken, described the different techniques being used: Chris Mackintosh stood upright, Bill Bracken leaned into a medium crouch, Emil Walch adopted the Arlberg Crouch, and Gustav Lantschner the Extreme Crouch. All the top racers of the day competed. Equipment was changing too. By the 2nd International Academic World Games in Davos in 1930, the Austrians had steel edges to their skis, though Bracken disdained them.

Controversy was important to Lunn. He used it constantly, of course, to fight the battle for downhill ski racing, but the lesson he had learnt at Harrow to use humour to convince his opponents still stood him in good stead. The same theme appeared in the Year Book. In his Review of the Year he wrote: "I am a great believer in controversy, provided it remains courteous and objective. In my support I can quote St Thomas Aquinas (Summa Theologica): 'In this way simple people are strengthened in the faith, and unbelievers are deprived of the opportunity to deceive, while if those who ought to withstand the perverters of truth were silent this would tend to strengthen error' ". Religion remained a strong influence in his life. The British Championships of 1931 were run early in January in Wengen by the

Downhill Only Club. Conditions were difficult, as snow was in short supply. Bill Bracken won for the third year in succession.

Immediately after the Championships, the racers crossed the Lauterbrunnen valley for the Roberts of Kandahar race on 13 January in Murren. There was an unfortunate incident. What snow there was had been beaten hard. Racers and organisers had been through days of hard racing too. With all racers setting off together in a geschmozzle start, there was the usual scramble over a steep and narrow turn aptly named 'Shambles Corner'. Peter Lunn arrived there last, but skied fast to take the lead and hold it until Martha's Gate, where he fell. Jimmy Riddell overtook him and maintained his lead through Martha's Meadow. He fell just above Beecher's Brook and on getting up looked around wildly for the finishing posts, which had no "Finish" banner between them. He shot past them, leaving Peter Lunn and Digby Raeburn, then 16 and 15 years old, to come first and second. Arnold Lunn said in his report that James Riddell "should have won but for his error of judgement".

Walter Amstutz was by this time working as Tourist Office Director in St Moritz, which he made into a World-class resort. He set the first "Flying Kilometre" there on 14 January 1931. It was a great success, won by Lantschner at what was then an astonishing speed of 105.675 kph. Another landmark that year was the first Lauberhorn Race, organised in Wengen in January by Ernst Gertsch.

The Arlberg-Kandahar that March was held in Murren for the first time. Hannes Schneider came for it and was awarded Honorary Membership of the Kandahar Ski Club. The World's best racers came for the race and Sigmund Ruud showed how well the Norwegians could adapt by winning the slalom. The downhill and combined were won by Otto 'Matterhorn' Furrer of Zermatt, through a combination of strength, stamina and bravery. Racers could choose their own line between the Schiltgrat and Gimmelwald, and Sigmund Ruud spent much of his time in the air. Audrey Sale-Barker ran everything straight and never fell, so winning both the downhill and slalom for the British ladies. "Sport", the Swiss tabloid, reported: "Today we have seen the finest downhill race that has ever taken place".

Lunn was still determined that the British should win. In the 1923 Year Book he had devoted a good deal of space to proving that the British racers at that time could take on the Swiss and beat them. He was delighted whenever the Anglo-Swiss races proved him right. Eventually however, British racers could no longer compete on equal terms with those born in the mountains. Many of Lunn's friends like Walter Amstutz had regularly skied to school and back every day throughout their childhood. They were naturally fitter and more expert as skiers. So Lunn began to think about races for those brought up in towns (he called them "citadins") or living in countries where there were no mountains. Lowlander races were to be run between the Belgians, the Danes, the Dutch and the British.

But in 1931 the British racers were still as good as any in the World. "Sport" devoted its whole front page to the British Ski Championship meeting in Wengen, and said it would be impossible to collect together as many good downhill racers in an event confined to the Swiss. Lunn, however, thought that by then their opinion of British racers was unjustifiably high. It was because we led the way in organising downhill racing that we had done so well.

The 1931 FIS Downhill was organised in Murren in February by the Ski Club of Great Britain and was later recognised as the first World Championships in Alpine racing. The downhills for both men and ladies were to be run in two races over the same course. Countries were given a quota of 6 racers each, as 36 was then considered the maximum entry for a downhill. The draw for the ladies race was held on 18 February and that for the men on 19 February.

The first half of the men's downhill, run to Winteregg, was held in the morning in a snowstorm. Lunn was pleased to note that those who used the Telemark position fared better than those who tried the Arlberg Crouch. The second half should have had a Hindmarsh start – with racers starting in the order in which they finished the first half. Because of the massive snowfalls this second half, due to be run on the Schiltgrat side that afternoon, had to be cancelled.

Another race was due to be held the following day on the full Schilthorn to Lauterbrunnen Inferno course, but only Grutsch to Lauterbrunnen could be used. Lunn did not really approve of changing the course because he felt that racers should contend with difficult weather but, as organiser, he listened to the other nations. It was held in ideal conditions. Gustavo Lantschner won overall, with Chris Mackintosh second (an accident earlier in the season had injured his hip), Bill Bracken was 7th, and James Riddell 10th. Neither the Poles nor the Italians came. An unofficial men's slalom was held the day after the meeting was over, by which time some competitors had left.

The British ladies were supreme, Esme Mackinnon at 16 won both downhills and the slalom. In the second downhill, which went through the trees to Lauterbrunnen, she was blocked almost at the end of the race by a funeral on the road near the Finish. Luckily the Swiss timekeeper saw her arriving and stopped his watch, starting it again for her to finish after the procession had passed. Count Bonacossa was Timekeeping Referee and accepted the combined time.

Lunn had completed his two years as President of the Ski Club of Great Britain, and retired at the Annual General Meeting. He could report that the Club was thriving, taking in 650 new members that year. He continued to chair the Technical Committee from 1931-1938 and remained on that Committee until 1958.

The 1931 British Ski Year Book contained a record 450 pages, including articles from important international figures such as Oestgaard and W.R. Rickmers, as well as old friends like Alan d'Egville who sent an amusing letter from Canada. Articles covered the world of skiing. F.S. Smythe contributed an account of his climb with Marcel Kurz on Kanchenjunga. Though they failed to reach the top, the climb was important as they took skis with them. Iceland and Japan were featured, as well as the Pyrenees, Colorado, Australia and the Tarentaise. It makes interesting reading now that those areas have been developed. Peisey Nancroit was then an isolated village, today it lies at the bottom of a busy run from Les Arcs. The area round Samoens, now networked by lifts and pistes into the huge Flaine area, was recommended as good touring country. The Equipment section also included useful advice on steel edges and a description of Kandahar slalom flags, which included a spring joint - reinvented as spring poles in the 1990s! Vivian Caulfeild, then in charge of the ski department at Fortnum & Mason, brought readers up to date with current techniques.

In keeping with the SCGB amalgamation of clubs, there were reports from the British Universities Ski Club, Down Hill Only, English Ski Club, Kandahar, Ladies Ski Club, Mardens, Villars Visitors, the University Ski Clubs of Oxford and Cambridge, and others. Gerald Seligman reported on an avalanche in the Aletschwald which had killed two ladies.

By 1930 Lunn had begun to change his views on Roman Catholicism. In the 1929 Year Book he had quoted Knox (now a Catholic priest) as saying: "The World is divided into those who take it or leave it and those who split the difference". They had started an exchange of letters on religious problems. The letters, written between 22 July 1930 and 5 October 1931, were published in a book called "Difficulties" in 1932. While the letters were being exchanged, Peter Lunn arrived home for a few days to find his father unusually preoccupied. On asking his mother why, he was told: "The terrible thing is that Ronald Knox seems to be winning".

1931 was another difficult year for the family firm. The recession meant foreign currency was limited and holidays abroad suffered. The Government issued an appeal for all those thinking of travelling abroad to stay at home instead. So hundreds who had booked with the Public Schools Alpine Sports Club cancelled their reservations. Henry Lunn faced ruin and Arnold did all he could to help, although he would have preferred to spend his time writing. In a letter to Geoffrey Winthrop Young, Arnold Lunn wrote: "I have been having a devil of a time recently, trying to save our firm from going into liquidation. It has been rather a tragic business. One rather disagreeable result is that if I succeed in reconstructing the company with new capital, I shall have to come back to England and devote a great deal more time to the business and less time to writing than I should like." He enlisted the help of his friend Christopher Mackintosh, the ski racer. At 27 Mackintosh was already an entrepreneur and he took over the firm, setting up a company named Alpine Sports Ltd., of which he became President and Arnold Lunn Managing Director. Lunn's knowledge of the people of Murren was invaluable. He was able to suggest who might invest money in the firm. Peter was sent to Mullheim in Baden to learn German. He was able to ski at weekends on the Feldberg and was asked to set a Kandahar slalom there.

By 1932 the recession was still hitting Britain. The Chancellor of the Exchequer again urged all patriotic Englishmen to stay at home, so the British Ski Championships were cancelled. But a full team of men and women went to Cortina for the FIS meeting - known that year as the European Ski Championship Meeting. The downhill for men, followed by that for the ladies, was held on 4 February. There were some problems with lack of snow and with spectators who crowded onto the course, hindering the ladies especially.

Roesli Streif, who was Ladies Alpine World champion that year, described in the 1968 Year Book how amateur the racers were in 1932. The only uniform for the Swiss Ladies was a team pullover and a headband - which they had to give back after the races. Racers had to walk for nearly three hours to reach the slalom - all the horse-drawn carriages were occupied by important guests, whose elaborate lunch was served by waiters in tailcoats. At the prize giving, racers who did not wear evening dress were refused entry.

The teams asked for slalom flags for training, and were given some which were so flimsy they broke. On returning the whole ones, they were told they had broken those intended for the race. Luckily Lois Butler, one of the racers, came to the rescue. Mrs Walter Amstutz telephoned her husband, who loaded his private plane with Kandahar flags and dropped them over Cortina. A number of unsuitable flagkeepers were replaced by more up-to-date escorts of the different teams. The

British Team were handicapped by not using wax in the downhill, but did well in the slalom.

The Fifth A-K was held at St Anton and Lunn was there. In deep snow, the Telemark was still used for straight running. Lunn recorded with regret that Peter was blinded by a fall of snow off a tree and shot off course and down a hole.

The Year Book included a very good article on snow deposits and the formation of cornices by Gerald Seligman. It was to become the basis of his classic work "Snow Structure and Ski Fields", which was the first authoritative work on avalanche prevention.

Lunn was writing industriously. "Family Name", one of the very few novels that he wrote, appeared that year. It drew heavily on his experiences in school at Harrow and on his skiing in Murren. Lunn wrote his own review in the Year Book.

A guidebook to "The Italian Lakes and Lakeland Cities" came out in the Kitbag Travel Books series, for which he had already written "Switzerland" and "Venice". But it was "Difficulties" - the exchange of letters with Ronald Knox, which really changed his life. Lunn threw himself into religion in the same way as he had taken on skiing. At the end of his life, when being interviewed for television, he was asked: "Your main interest is skiing?" and replied, "No, my main interest throughout my life has been religion". In the same pattern of exchanging letters he started a correspondence with Professor Joad.

The 1932 Olympic Games at Lake Placid were covered very briefly in the British Ski Year Book's Review of the Year. They were the last Winter Games that featured only Nordic racing. The FIS Congress was held in Paris and professionalism was discussed. Lunn still wanted ski-teachers to be allowed to compete, though he was against big money prizes and gate money.

By now Lunn was no longer spending the summers in Grindelwald, but returning to Suttoncroft, in Bickley, Kent. In winter he stayed at The Palace Hotel in Murren. He was on good terms with other authors, lunching with

H.G. Wells in August. He also enjoyed meeting and corresponding with W.A.B. Coolidge, who shared his interest in mountaineering and writing.

The influence of the Kandahar was growing and the Canadians ran a Quebec Kandahar in 1932. The Infante Alfonso, father of three young Spanish princes, Alvaro, Alfonso and Ataulfo, who visited Murren, accepted Honorary Membership of the Kandahar. Lunn had been working on a small booklet entitled "Skiing in a Fortnight", which was published by Methuen in 1933. In it he aimed to enable the beginner to master the basic techniques of skiing in two weeks. He strongly discouraged the inclination to regard turns as an end in themselves, but they were a regrettable necessity. The real problem of skiing, he summed up in the short ugly word "funk", and he encouraged his readers to enter races in order to overcome it.

There was a notable paragraph in the chapter on equipment, which was headed: "Advice which will not be taken". It told the beginner to buy the best long skis he could afford, then hire an old short pair and practise the Stem turn and Stem Christiania until they were mastered. Then the reader would be ready to ski on his own good long pair. Telemark, jump turns and climbing uphill were all covered.

Peter was working for the Standard Motor Company, but managed to get time off to train for the FIS and a long weekend to compete in the A-K.

The 1933 FIS meeting was held in Innsbruck in very difficult and dangerous conditions. There was not enough snow and the track became a thin ribbon, strewn with tree stumps. Flu also hit the racers. Peter missed the team race because of it and all the ladies suffered for a week before the downhill, but bravely carried on. By this time it had been accepted that the weather was always bad for the FIS races. FIS-Im-Sturm, Lunn wrote, as opposed to Auf-Klarung giving fine weather for the A-K.

That year the A-K was in Murren. Because it had been warm, they could not use the usual A-K course from Schiltgrat to Gimmelwald, but instead raced down the Kandahar face. Ernst Gertsch came over from Wengen to help set the ladies slalom.

On 13 July 1933 Arnold was received into the Catholic Church by his old adversary Knox. He had been searching for religion and had finally found it. For the rest of his life it was to dominate his interest and work. That year in November, "Now I See" was published by Sheed & Ward, explaining the reasons for his conversion and tracing his journey from boyhood. It was to convert many to Catholicism.

He also published an exchange of letters with Cyril Joad entitled "Is Christianity True?" In Joad's last letter he paid tribute to Lunn's courtesy: "You have been eloquent, alert and amusing and you have hit hard and clean. I respect your intelligence, and I acknowledge an expert in the art of controversy".

Lunn's Secretary, Nora Williams, left to get married and Mabel told Arnold that she had found the perfect successor - the niece of a friend of hers. Lunn duly interviewed Phyllis Holt-Needham. He asked first if she knew shorthand and she admitted she was bad at it. "Doesn't matter," Lunn replied, "I use a Dictaphone." Pause. "Do you drive a car?" "Not very well". "Doesn't matter, I haven't got one." Pause. "Well thank you for calling. I'll write later." "You're not going to engage her on that", said Nora Williams. "I'm not engaging her", replied Lunn, "she's engaging me. I hope I give satisfaction".

It was indeed a very satisfactory appointment. Though 5 years later Phyllis Holt-Needham took on a war job, she returned afterwards as Assistant Editor of the Year Book. Quiet and unassuming, she was firm in keeping Lunn's papers - and indeed later his life - in order. A good judge of character, whereas he was often carried away by first impressions, she saved him from many pitfalls.

Writing later, Phyllis Holt-Needham recalled: "When I think back to my first winters in Murren, it is chiefly at the big round table just inside the dining room doors at the Palace that I remember Mabel. All through the season people came and went. Some had been coming there for years and took their places as of right. Others came for some special occasion and were asked to stay on; some were brought in when it was discovered that the rest of their party had gone home. However large the table became, Mabel always remained in complete control of it, and made a very cheerful party of every meal."

Lunn was by then well known in literary circles. He exchanged many friendly letters with Evelyn Waugh, who visited him and Mabel at Suttoncroft, and borrowed a book by Antonia White. Maurice Baring wrote to congratulate Lunn on becoming a Catholic - he had read "Difficulties" and "The Harrovians".

In the 1933 Year Book, Gerald Seligman's analysis of snow movement and causes of avalanches covered 150 well-illustrated pages. And he also contributed the Equipment section - 40 pages on skis, sticks, skins, boots, rucksacks, snow shovels, even cameras and compasses, avalanche sounding sticks, and rescue sledges.

Professor Mehl contributed an article on Zdarsky's slalom, which used gates. Arnold said: "The distinction between a controlled race and a slalom is surely this - In the race, the 'gates' are placed less to test the competitor's power to turn, where it is least convenient for him to turn, than to force the racer to turn at a convenient spot, in order to prevent crash racing." Caulfield supplied an article on Stem, Christiania and Stem-Christiania turns.

Peter won the Roberts of Kandahar in 1934. The main FIS events had become a battleground of nations, while the A-K remained a race that most competitors enjoyed. The Anglo-Swiss University races were equally popular. Lunn was to write nostalgically: "I look back again at an Anglo-Swiss Dinner and there is Deggers, and Werner with his concertina, and Tony Knebworth trying to jodel and Christopher singing a very low song in Bernese German". Sir Claud Schuster, President of the SCGB, referred in his Annual General Meeting Address to the fact that the Club's Editors were indispensable members of Council. In future they were coopted yearly.

Much of Lunn's writing now concerned religious themes including "A Saint in the Slave Trade", which was the life of St Peter Claver (1581-1654). In 1935 "Science & the Supernatural", written with J.S. Haldane, was published. It was to have an influence on both Phyllis Holt-Needham and Lord Longford.

The FIS Council met in Sweden in 1935 and Lunn travelled from St Moritz with Dr. Minelle, the FIS Vice President. He was met on the platform in Stockholm with a bouquet of tulips. Both Colonel Holmquist and Count Hamilton called at his hotel in Solleftea to welcome him. Czechoslovakia was proposed to host the 1936 FIS race, but Lunn disagreed as he did not think they had either the expertise or the courses to provide good downhill and slalom races. In a wonderfully witty speech he persuaded the Council to allow Britain to organise the downhill and slalom in 1936, leaving the cross-country, jumping and other events to the Czechs. He was elected a member of FIS Council.

The FIS downhill race meeting started in St Moritz on 15 February 1935. Jimmy Riddell, who had been out of skiing for a year, turned up just as the training was beginning and Lunn said he was skiing brilliantly. Then during the race both he and Birnie Duthie of the British Team were blocked on the wood path for half a minute. As a result, it was agreed that numbers should be drawn in future and start intervals increased to a minute. Lunn set the slalom at Walter Amstutz's invitation, and Ernst Gertsch helped him. Chris Mackintosh and Peter Lunn were appointed by the SCGB Council as Captain and Vice-Captain of the British Team, but Mackintosh later resigned because he was unable to join the Team during training, so Peter Lunn was promoted to Captain. Arnold Lunn was not at the Arlberg-Kandahar. He had had some altercations with the Austrian Nazis. The Ladies Race was won by Jeannette Kessler. Lunn wrote: "I am inclined to believe that Miss Kessler is the most stylish and perhaps the best lady runner that I so far have had the fortune to watch on the snows". Holland was represented for the first time and Baroness Schimmelpennink van de Oye was to cooperate with Lunn in developing races for those not born in the mountains. Evie Pinching, who had been trained by Bill Bracken, finished 5th. Helen Blane of the Kandahar just failed to qualify, finishing 12th.

At the International Downhill and Slalom races in Riksgransen, Sweden, Lt. Siegfried Bergman, who had raced downhill for the first time in the Parsenn and A-K that year, ran the course Hors Concours at an average speed of 60kph. He also set the slalom. Sigge Bergman was later to act as Secretary of the FIS for many years. Helen Blane was officially entered and finished 5th in the combined, which Lunn described as a fine performance. She went on to win the Polish Championships.

The Infante Alfonso and his family again spent the winter of 1935 in Murren, where the World Championships were held. The three Princes were excellent ski racers and Lunn wrote to ask the Spanish Federation to enter them, which they did to the surprise of the Infanta Beatrice. She had been convinced that the Republican Government would never allow Spain to be represented by Royal exiles. The Spanish Federation insisted on the Princes belonging to a club, so they joined the Penalara Club. Sadly there was a sequel when the Civil War broke out and Senor Jose Guilera and fellow members of the Penalara Club were all imprisoned as monarchists.

In the autumn of 1935, Lunn was invited to the United States to lecture on apologetics. The occasion was chaired by Father Purcell, Editor of "The Sign", a famous American Catholic paper. The lecture was a great success and was to lead to a 30-year assignment. Lunn always felt at home in the United States and made many friends there.

8

1936-39 Against Totalitarianism!

Lunn wrote of the 1936 Olympics: "The snows of Garmisch were flecked by the shadows of war". He was bitterly opposed to the Nazi regime and, although these should have been triumphant Olympics for him because for the first time downhill and slalom were included, he was deeply unhappy because they were organised by the Nazis, whose influence was overpowering. Contemporary film shows the streets lined with swastikas and soldiers everywhere.

He was reluctant even to go to Garmisch-Partenkirchen, but he had been appointed referee for the men's slalom and his son Peter was Captain of the British Team. So he went, but when the Games were opened by Adolf Hitler neither he nor Peter walked in the march-past.

The remainder of the British Team marched through the sleet but, like the French, carefully gave the Olympic rather than the Nazi salute. This meant stretching the arm out to the side rather than forward. It was difficult, though, when marching closely together and one of the British girls flung her arm sideways with such force that it hit the nose of her neighbour. Even so, some of the spectators thought the British were giving the Nazi salute and greeted them with cheers rather than the silence that greeted the Americans, who did not salute at all.

The only medal awarded for alpine skiing was for the combined. In the strained atmosphere, the British did not shine. James Riddell crashed in the downhill and was unable to compete in the slalom. Peter Lunn was steady, but uncharacteristically slow. Jeannette Kessler and Evie Pinching came 8th and 9th in the ladies combined. But even Arnold Lunn had to agree that the organisation was superb. The choice and preparation of the courses, the setting of the slaloms and the planning of the news service all ran smoothly. Journalists had their own press hut with telegraph and post office; doctors and surgeons gave their services free.

In spite of this, Lunn did not think that skiing should remain an Olympic sport. He thought that events that carry great publicity and prestige were a menace to the spirit of the sport. The only way to preserve the friendly traditions was to keep skiing out of anything sufficiently important to merit headlines in the Press or an official banquet. (Very much the same attitude was taken by snowboarders after the 1998 Olympics.)

The FIS Congress that year met in Garmisch and the British proposal to allow the FIS downhill race, which they were about to organise, to be run as a World Championship event was accepted. So, a week after the Olympics, Lunn arrived in Innsbruck to prepare for the Alpine World Championships. Though neither referee nor course setter, he was, of course, on the Race Committee. He found to his alarm that the course had been prepared on the slope that had proved so dangerous in 1933. On the Mutters side, it was too low with the finish below 600m. On race day a heavy thaw had melted most of the snow, then a sharp frost turned what was left into sheet ice. The worst part was about 150m above the finish, where a very steep slope led to a long glade with a narrow ribbon of snow about 4m wide. This glade contained a succession of bumps, jerking the skier onto the tree stumps that lined each side.

The race was postponed for an hour and Lunn said afterwards that not postponing it altogether was the worst blunder in his skiing career. Out of 54 starters there were 17 casualties. Racers and spectators became hysterical, women fainted, men swore at the organisers. A row of men were posted towards the finish, to catch women as they hit the bumps with a resounding whack and hurtled down across a mixture of snow and earth towards the trees.

The British Team rose to the occasion. Evie Pinching skied magnificently to win the Ladies Championship. Peter Lunn nicely judged a mixture of bravery and control to come 9th in the Men's Downhill.

At St Anton for the Arlberg-Kandahar, Lunn rejoiced in the change of atmosphere after the sinister clouds of Germany. He wrote that year of Schneider: "Perhaps it is the personality of Hannes which is more responsible than any other single factor for the A-K atmosphere. The ten years that have passed since Walter Bernays introduced me to Hannes have only served to deepen my respect and affection for this paladin of skiing. He dominates St Anton, not only in virtue of his outstanding success as a teacher and his great record as an active skier, but by force of his engaging personality. His leadership is a leadership of character and there is a granite-like integrity about the man which is unaffected by the vacillations of political fashion."

There was a big entry, and reading through the results one comes across many of those who were to have a big influence on skiing in the years to come. Emile Allais was to design courses in resorts all over the World. Friedl Pfeiffer set up ski schools in America; Rudi Matt took over the direction of the Arlberg Ski School after the war; Baroness Schimmelpennick van der Oye was to develop Citadin and Lowlander racing with Lunn and guide the Netherlands into racing.

Of the British, Audrey Sale-Barker, Jeannette Kessler and Helen Blane were to have a big influence on British ski-racing, with Helen (who married Bill Tomkinson) becoming one of the very few women Honorary Members of the FIS.

Lunn was intensely competitive, but did not expect that to detract from the enjoyment of racing. He was against big-money prizes, which would turn each race into work for the racer. He did not, either, want racing to become nationalistic. Those entered in the Arlberg-Kandahar raced for their clubs. He discouraged a lot of flag-waving and anthem-singing at prize givings. The FIS races were becoming more and more serious, which he thought was because competitors raced for their countries.

By 1936 he had worked out rules for those who lived in towns rather than mountains – citadins rather than berglers. He had intended to run an event for these citadins in 1936, and even had a cup called after the Kandahar's patron, the Duke of Kent. However, the death of George V meant that the first event of this kind had to be put off until 1937.

With the Olympics, World Championships and the British Championships (run in Wengen), 1936 was an action-packed season. Even so, Lunn found time to join ski tours organised by the Eagle Ski Club. On 1 April he was back in London to give a lecture to SCGB members on the Olympic Games and the FIS.

Steel edges were becoming more common – Ernst Gertsch had had them fitted to his skis three years before and found they prevented wear and gave no trouble. But the increasing rigidity of bindings was causing many injuries. While attending the Grand Prix de Megeve, Lunn tried out a new binding, which released the foot in a lateral twist. It had been invented locally and was recommended by Emile Allais.

G.K. Chesterton died in June and Lunn wrote to Hilaire Belloc, saying: "You and Chesterton have been the two biggest influences in my life since, as an undergraduate, I read your 'Path to Rome' and 'Orthodoxy'. To you and to him I owe, under God, my faith." Other close friends made at this time were Douglas Woodruff, a Catholic writer, and his wife Mia. Lunn was a welcome guest at their house in Stanford Dingley.

The Year Book included a special 46-page section on the Olympics. Always ready to admit to his own failings, Lunn told readers that they would have had some odd surprises, but for the careful proof-reading of Colonel Bowdler. Peter Lunn took over the Equipment section from Gerald Seligman, who had also retired as Editor of "Ski Notes & Queries", though he continued to write scholarly articles on snow conditions and avalanche prevention.

In 1936, Lunn started a three-year assignment lecturing on apologetics each autumn at the University of Notre Dame in the United States. For three days each week he lectured on Hellenism and Christianity. Lunn wrote to his mother saying he felt like an undergraduate lecturing to graduates. He found them less bumptious than those at Oxford. He was now well-known to skiers and both the Ski Dreiverein Club of New York and the Appalachian Club of Boston entertained him. Walter Bernays was in New York at the time.

While he was in the States, the Pittsburgh Community Forum persuaded a prominent communist, Earl Browder, to debate with him. At the last moment Earl Browder pleaded an excuse and was replaced by another communist, Luis Budenz, who was so convinced by Lunn's arguments that he was converted to Catholicism.

The Anglo-Swiss University races were held on 31 December 1936 in St Moritz, where Walter Amstutz was still the Tourist Office Director. The British Open Championship meeting was held in January at Grindelwald. It was not really a success as an open race and it was decided to run it for British racers only in future. The Tenth A-K was held in Murren.

The first Duke of Kent Cup for "citadins" was run in Murren on 9 January 1937, and was an immediate success with over 90 entries. The spirit, as well as the letter of the rules was kept when some entries voluntarily withdrew although strictly they could have qualified. One was Peter Lunn, who had spent a lot of his life in the mountains, and another was Marc Hodler who had had the benefit of his family's holiday chalet in Murren. Hodler says he was told firmly by Lunn that he was a "bergler", so could not compete in citadin races.

The race was won by young Arnold Kaech from Bern, whose team won the Infante Alfonso Cup for the town teams race. Kaech was later to work as Secretary General of the FIS for many years. He was a Brigadier in the Swiss Army, their highest rank, and for 22 years was the equivalent of a British Permanent Undersecretary at the Swiss Ministry of Defence, as well as serving as Military Attache in Sweden. Spending his later years in Murren, he was made President of the Schilthorn lift company.

The 1937 FIS meeting was held in Chamonix and Lunn arrived there to vet the courses on 8 February, a week before the downhill. He recalled that in 1897 he had walked up the Brevent on foot and a year later had skied there for the first time in his life. He was surprised to find that Payot, the pioneer of skiing in Chamonix, had started only one year before him.

When he came to inspect the Piste des Glaciers, the course agreed by the FIS Downhill Racing Committee, he decided it was dangerous, with many hidden rocks likely to trip up racers when turning. Ernst Gertsch inspected it with him and agreed. Although many trees had been chopped down, the lower stretches forced the racer to turn too often, without places where brave racers could point their skis straight down the hill. Lunn had to insist that the course be moved from the one on which Chamonix had spent so much money. On the day of the race, six holiday skiers broke their legs on the Piste des Glaciers. If the race had not been moved to another slope, there would have been far more casualties among the racers.

There was a scratch British Team because Peter Lunn had injured his back, Aitchison had flu and an injured ankle, and Palmer-Tomkinson was working for his school finals. Evie Pinching and Jeannette Kessler were in India. Doreen Elliott came as manager of the British girls. Heavy snow fell before and during the race.

After his experiences at Innsbruck and Chamonix, Lunn decided that courses should be inspected in summer when it was possible to see what rocks lay under the snow. On 2 February he sent a formal letter to Oestgaard about the necessity to approve safe courses, which had been viewed by the FIS in the summer. He even specified that the ski association desiring one of its courses to be inspected should pay the second-class fare of an expert appointed to do this job. The idea was accepted by the FIS, which then issued a yearly list of courses approved - or as they call them homologated - for various events all over the World.

Now, at last, the Alpine Club elected Lunn a member. He was proposed by Charles Schuster and seconded by Leo Amery. Among his supporters were Aldo Bonacossa, Winthrop Young and Bentley Beauman. Lord Schuster, who had earlier been President of the SCGB, was determined that this time there should be no refusal. He told the Committee that if Lunn was blackballed again from ordinary membership, the Committee would award him honorary membership, so anyone blackballing him would only lead to him being given a higher honour. When elected, Lunn congratulated the Club on "opening the stable door once the horse was in".

In 1937 Lunn went to cover the Spanish Civil War as a reporter for the Catholic papers The Universe and The Tablet. He wrote home regularly with news of battles, typically understating the dangers. In one letter he wrote: "We are shepherded round the Front like a Cooks tour. Or a Lunn tour". He was, however, often in the front line and experienced bombing and shelling.

One day, planes overhead threatened them on the road. Lunn wrote to Mabel: "Remembering that the Reds never fly low enough to machine gun a road, and holding firm to my principle that the bulls eye is the safest spot on the target at which the Red planes are aiming, I did not follow the Germans into the field, but looked round for a ditch by the road. But, before ruining the tweed suit which you hate, I could neither see nor hear them so we returned to the car." He would send long reports back and ask that Phyllis Holt-Needham should copy and distribute them.

His links with the Spanish Royal Family gave him a good understanding of their predicament and a strong dislike of the communists. The Infante Alfonso was second in command of the Nationalist Air Force and his three sons all fought in the air. Alonso was killed near Granada in the first month of the war. Ataulfo was in an air accident the same day, but survived. Alvaro, Lunn described as "a real conquistador type who adored his job of bombing". Always admiring bravery, Lunn contrasted the monarchists who dived down low to hit their targets accurately, with the communists who, scared of anti-aircraft fire, remained high in the sky and missed their targets. The Infanta Beatrice worked with the sick and poor at Lerida. Lunn often stayed in their Palace. He wrote a book about his experiences, called "Spanish Rehearsal".

While he was in the States in 1937, Lunn also lectured to Dartmouth College, which took up downhill and slalom racing and was instrumental in introducing them to the States.

The Anglo-Swiss University Races started 1938 well with exciting courses at Murren on 5 January. Marc Hodler won the slalom and combined, with Arnold Kaech third in the slalom and the British saved from ignominy by Jimmy Palmer-Tomkinson, who came third in the combined.

The British Ski Championships were run by the Kandahar in Murren on 11-12 January 1938, just after the Duke of Kent Cup. There had been a long period of severe cold just before Christmas, which was ended by a thaw setting in just before mid-January. The Lauberhorn Cup was held in Wengen on 15-16 January.

Lunn left Murren on Wednesday 16 February, to cross six frontiers before arriving at Helsinki on the 19th for the FIS Congress. In Basle he met Count Aldo Bonacossa, who represented Italy, and they travelled together. At the Congress there were various problems, some of which were connected with the political situation. Austria had lost its representation since the Anschluss; Finland and Czechoslovakia both had ambiguous representation.

A great deal of time was spent debating the amateur situation with regard to the next Olympics, scheduled for 1940. It was finally agreed to withdraw from the Olympics unless the International Olympic Committee agreed to accept the FIS definition of an amateur, i.e. ski instructors could qualify but not those who went in for big money prizes.

The World Championships in downhill ski racing were held at Engelberg with the straight race on 4 March. Conditions were rugged for training, with a steep narrow path down which racers had to speed and Marc Hodler was nearly killed when he fell in training, breaking a leg and piercing a vein.

Lunn described as "very beautiful" the swift succession of first-class racers following each other down the big schuss. Seen today on film, the racers, with flapping ski-trousers and long unwieldy skis look brave rather than beautiful. Schneider was in Engelberg and announced to a group of friends that Austria would never become German. A fortnight later Germany had annexed Austria and Schneider was in prison. The eleventh Arlberg-Kandahar was due to be held at St Anton on 19-20

March. Lunn was in Rome and when the British Team reached St Anton they found that Schneider had been arrested by the Nazis. The Team sent Lunn a telegram, which, as they did not know where he was staying, they addressed "care of the Pope, Rome." It duly reached him and he left at once for St Anton.

Schneider, though not a Jew himself, had always been anti-Nazi and some time before had sacked one of his ski instructors, Moser, because he was pro-Nazi. Moser had now been appointed Burgermeister of St Anton.

Lunn called first on Dr Rudolph Gomperz, President of the Arlberg Ski Club, who had always been so helpful, and announced that he would cancel the Arlberg-Kandahar. Gomperz protested and Lunn realised that, as a Jew, he too was in danger of reprisals from the Nazis. So Lunn said he would tell everyone that Gomperz had done his very best to persuade the Kandahar to hold the race. This exonerated Gomperz, but even so he was later sent to Vienna and then disappeared in the Holocaust. His Will, a poignant testimony to his banishment, is recorded today in the museum at St Anton.

Lunn summoned a meeting of the members of the Kandahar, among whom were several Americans. They decided unanimously to cancel the A-K, and a subcommittee, which included Betty Woolsey, Mervyn Thomas, Jimmy Palmer-Tomkinson, Arnold and Peter Lunn, wrote to the Arlberg Ski Club. It was decided that the A-K would not be run again until Schneider had returned to St Anton in his old job. Meanwhile an international Kandahar race would be held in March 1939 in Murren.

A member of the Arlberg Ski Club scolded Lunn for "mixing up politics and sport". In reply Lunn asked if Schneider had been imprisoned because he skied badly. Lunn then called on Moser and told him the race was to be cancelled unless Schneider was returned to his former job.

Lunn is often credited with persuading the Nazis to release Hannes Schneider by refusing to run the A-K, and there is no doubt that he played an important part. He himself said that he was one among many people who had some influence on the Nazis and appealed to them to allow Schneider to leave for the United States.

Benno Rybiska, a ski instructor trained by Schneider, was running the Eastern Slope Ski School, billed as the American Branch of the Hannes Schneider School, in North Conway, New Hampshire. Harvey Gibson, a rich American, owned the principal hotel there. Alice Kiare, another American who used to bring the United States Ladies Team to St Anton and house them in a chalet at the bottom of the course, contacted Gibson. He offered Schneider a job. It was also rumoured that he used his influence to put off repayment of debts owed by the Nazis to his bank. But Schneider promised not to reveal the details of this arrangement and the promise was kept. It was certainly Harvey Gibson who provided Schneider's wife and children with tickets and arranged for them to pick up Hannes from Karl Roesen's chalet in Garmisch-Partenkirchen and travel on to the States.

In April, Lunn was in Spain watching the final battles of the Spanish Civil War. He spent Easter, and his 50th birthday, at Epila, headquarters of the Spanish Air Force, with the Infante and Infanta d'Orleans-Bourbon. He wrote to Mabel, saying he had met British prisoners-of-war. "The Reds were anti-religious, killing priests and nuns". In August, he wrote to his mother about meeting the Queen of Spain: "A jolly vivacious person with any amount of fun".

In 1938, after lecturing at Notre Dame as Assistant Professor of Apologetics, Lunn travelled through Canada and also explored the US North-West, visiting Mount Hood and Yosemite, which he thought were destined to play a great part in the future of skiing. Once when lecturing he was introduced as the author of "Guide to Montana" and the audience took that to be Montana USA. He did not disillusion them.

Like his father, he wanted to bring various religions together, so one evening he invited a Rabbi, a Methodist parson, a journalist, and a young atheist to dinner. He kept in touch with his friends, writing one day to Etta Bonacossa, wife of his friend Aldo, to let her know he was lecturing in the States.

The 1938 Year Book continued the tradition of important and multinational contributors. There was an article on skis by the Norwegian ski historian Helge Refsum. He had contributed a valuable collection of ancient skis to the Ski Club of Great Britain, who proudly displayed them in their clubhouse. Kenya and New Zealand featured also.

King Albert of the Belgians, a great lover of mountaineering, had watched the Anglo-Swiss races and met Walter Amstutz there. They often climbed together without a guide. The King invited Arnold and Mabel to stay at the Chateau de Laaken, where he returned from a day scrambling on the pinnacles of the Meuse. He was later to die climbing by himself.

The Anglo-Swiss races in St Moritz on 27 December 1938 were won by the British for the first time since 1933 – though the individual combined winner was Marc Hodler. The Duke of Kent Cup was held in Wengen on 9 January. British skiers did slightly better than in the previous year and the event itself was a great success, consisting of a straight race with an outright championship and a team race of four from each town who competed for a challenge cup.

The Annual General Meeting of the Ski Club of Great Britain was held on 6 July. Brian Meredith took over from Alan d'Egville as Editor of Ski Notes & Queries. Miss Cave, invaluable Secretary of the Club, retired. Colonel Sturmy Cave, who had been Honorary Secretary, also resigned. Both jobs were combined and Kenneth Smith became the new Secretary of the Club and was to see it through the war. Sir Roger Keyes took over from Rear Admiral Bromley as President. Lunn handed over the Chair of the SCGB's Technical Committee, which he had held since its foundation in 1921. He spent much of the summer in Italy and compiled the Year Book there.

In 1939 Lunn was again asked by the Nazi Sport Leader to run an A-K at St Anton. He said afterwards that his carefully worded reply might have been interpreted as a promise to bring the A-K back to St Anton if Schneider were allowed to leave for the States. After he had done so Salcher, the Nazi Sport Leader, asked if they could meet to discuss the date of the resumed Arlberg-Kandahar.

Lunn was by then travelling through Austria en route for Zakopane to help with the organisation of the World Ski Championships – the tenth anniversary of Zakopane's first international downhill. Lunn suggested that

Salcher should join the train, where they could discuss the A-K. A hopeful Salcher got into the train in St Anton, but was told the Kandahar still refused to resume relations with him or the Nazified Arlberg Ski Club. "But you promised that you would bring back the Arlberg-Kandahar in your letter to our Sport Leader". Lunn had a copy of his letter and said that though they had released Schneider, they must now get rid of Hitler.

At Zakopane, the Poles invited him to chair the race committee and referee both the downhill and slalom. He deplored the zenophobia – there were national anthems, national teams and a strong political feeling. Lunn proposed Ella (Kini) Maillart, a well-known Swiss explorer, to the committee.

He was particularly absentminded at this time. He travelled to Poland with the British Ladies Team. Helen Tomkinson (then Blane) remembered the journey well. The train was packed and as there was only one sleeper she and the other girls sat up all night. They had to change trains in Vienna and when they reached the train for Poland, Lunn found he had left his luggage in the sleeper. She was detailed to fetch it, almost missing the connection herself. Then at breakfast he appeared with his trousers on inside-out. It was easy to do, he reported in the Year Book, for with the elastic round the ankles you pull them off and then climb in again the next morning.

On arrival at Zakopane, the British were met by sleighs with Poles wearing big fur hats and jackets – it was a romantic welcome. Germany and Austria were represented by just one team. Many racers resented the Anschluss, so would not talk to the Germans. The Austrians, however, did well and Lunn said that the true winner was the lonely Schneider, now in America. He also took Jimmy Palmer-Tomkinson and Helen Blane to the race meetings, introducing them to race organisation. He had a fierce battle at the meeting with the Germany's Baron Le Fort. Lunn chaired the Downhill-Slalom Committee of the FIS at the World Championships.

An Alpine Kandahar was held that year in Murren, as a substitute for the Arlberg-Kandahar, but Lunn had to return to England the day before the race because his father was dying. Sir Henry Lunn had been fit up to four months earlier, when he was reported to be in excellent form as a guest at the Alpine Ski Club's 30th Anniversary Dinner. But he died in March 1939, leaving just £66 and a small annuity for his wife.

Lunn was making many friends among writers and skiers in the States. Roland Palmedo became an Honorary Member of the SCGB in 1938. Nathaniel Goodrich and Professor Hildebrand of California contributed information about the history of skiing in the US. The 1939 Duke of Kent Cup was held in January and the British Championships were organised that year by the Down Hill Only Club in Wengen on 12-13 January. Isobel Roe, who was to have a big influence on British skiing after the war, won for the second year in succession. James and Helen Palmer-Tomkinson – brother and sister – won the straight races.

Lunn explained why he must be controversial. An Editor, he wrote, may be compared to a bee. If you remove the sting, the bee dies.

It was at about this time that Lunn betrayed a good visual memory. Sitting in the train in Wengen, he saw a man wearing a K badge. Admitting that he could not remember names but recognised the wearer, he spoke to him. It turned out to be Prince Bernhard of the Netherlands.

9

1939-45 WORLD WAR II

LUNN RETURNED TO England from Italy just before the outbreak of war and after six weeks left for the Balkans as occasional correspondent of a New York weekly paper. On his way through from Belgrade to Bucharest he spent a week in Budapest, where Owen O'Malley was British Ambassador.

It had been in O'Malley's rooms at Magdalen College, Oxford that the proposal had first been made to found the Alpine Ski Club. O'Malley invited leading Hungarian skiers to dinner to meet Lunn and a postcard to Baron Le Fort, then Nazi Ski Leader, was handed round for signatures and messages.

Lunn left the Balkans in the middle of December and spent Christmas in Rome. All the experiences he had accumulated on his travels went into a book entitled "Whither Europe?" On Boxing Day he went to Murren, feeling very nostalgic about his time there during World War I.

He left the Bernese Oberland towards the end of February to lecture for the British Council in Malta, Palermo, Naples and Rome. Peter Lunn had been posted to Malta, with his wife Antoinette and baby David, so he was able to see them. Switzerland was expecting an invasion, so Lunn went back to Scheidegg to collect his luggage, and have a farewell lunch with Walter Hofmann at the Hotel du Lac in Interlaken.

He reached Paris on 16 May, carrying the Legation bag. His absent-mindedness was now well-known and when taking the bag he had insisted it would reach its destination. "I have a very untidy outside, but a very tidy inside. I classify things into those I can lose, such as hats and overcoats, and things I can't, such as passports, passes and Legation bags". The friend who handed over the bag did not find this very reassuring. "I was told in Budapest", he said, "that a Romanian Attache had a Legation bag stolen on the way through to Bucharest. He shot himself. We should, of course, expect you to shoot yourself if the bag goes astray." "Unfortunately", came Lunn's reply, "this is one of those rare cases where ecclesiastical and diplomatic etiquette seem to clash." Back home in Kent, he felt restless. Britain was not as familiar as Switzerland.

During the war he travelled constantly, lecturing for the British Council. The official subject of his talks was the influence of sport on society, beginning with the classical Olympic Games. But, especially when he was in America, he was persuading his audience to support Britain in the war. Often he would start the lecture by asking everyone whether they would prefer to hear about the blitz. They always did. A frequent theme was anti-totalitarianism, against Nazis, Fascists and Communists.

When lecturing he was patient, thorough and always amusing. He appealed to sportsmen and to co-religionists. His wit and his kind and swift ripostes won support. Even his vanity was good-natured and self- deprecating. Typically he said of himself: "When it comes to humility, I'm tops".

He recognised that the British Ski Year Book could be good propaganda and was determined to continue its publication throughout the war. He was pleased when, in 1942, the Oregon Journal wrote: "After two years of war, during which the Club's headquarters were damaged by bombs and hostile armies have separated England from her ski grounds in the Alps, the SCGB lives on, and makes plans for the annual Year Book. It is an example and a challenge."

The annual was filled with anti-Nazi propaganda – including an account of the horrors that were going on in Dachau prison. There were reminiscences, book reviews, accounts of skiing in Britain, obituaries and news of racers. For example, Mouse Cleaver, who had won the first Lauberhorn race, was reported to have lost his sight for some time, but later regained it in one eye. A record was kept of SCGB members killed in action or awarded medals for gallantry.

Lunn managed through his contributors to capture the beauty of the mountains and the fascination of snow. He did not lose contact with his friends. Both Walter Amstutz and his English wife Eveline contributed articles. Eveline, as Lunn learnt later (though not, he said, from her), helped prisoners of war to escape across the Swiss frontier.

Arguments still raged in print about ski technique. In the 1940 British Ski Year Book, Barry Caulfeild, son of Vivian, was still saying the Telemark might return, and warning readers not to specialise in the Christiania, which he wrote was a waste of time for beginners.

In 1940 Lunn visited Ireland as special correspondent of The Tablet. "Come What May", a first autobiography, was published that year. On 5 June Lunn stayed a night with Hugh Dowding, one-time SCGB rep and helper with race organisation, now Commander-in-Chief of Fighter Command. Lunn wanted to fly out to France to report the battle for an American paper and the Ministry of Information had backed his request. "I won't put a spoke in your wheel," said Dowding, "but I think you're a mutt. You'll have to be a Scarlet Pimpernel to get back from France." He predicted that France would fall within two weeks – a remarkably accurate prediction as Lunn said, for 12 days later the French asked for an armistice. John Lunn was among those successfully evacuated from Dunkirk. Several times Lunn sat in Dowding's room at Fighter Command from 9pm until 1 or 2am. Churchill nearly always rang about midnight. During that summer Lunn also spent a night with a group of fighter pilots.

At the end of October 1940, he sailed from England and arrived in New York on election day, 5 November, to make a four-month lecture tour. He dined on arrival with Robert Wilberforce of the British Library of Information. Lunn was very sensitive about being out of Britain during the war and uneasy at being away from danger, but when much later he was knighted for work in the skiing world and Anglo-Swiss relations,

Robert Wilberforce wrote: "Far more important was the work you did for Anglo-American relations at truly difficult times and against the most tremendous odds."

From November to March he travelled over 25,000 miles, crossing the United States twice from coast to coast. He shuttled north to Halifax, south to Miami and lectured to Catholics, Protestants, Jews, Rotarians, ski clubs, British war-relief societies, dons and undergraduates. In all, he was in 20 countries during the war, crossed the Atlantic six times and spent some months in South America.

There were, of course, some opportunities to meet old skiing friends. In New York, the Palmedos had collected several of them together. Alice Kiare brought Hannes Schneider from North Conway and he arrived wearing the A-K Founders Badge, which both he and Lunn had been awarded.

Lunn was spending a week lecturing at Loretto Heights College in Denver when he heard of the Coventry raids. The Americans were very kind. His published theme that day was mountaineering and skiing, but he also showed some slides of the Battle of Britain and said it would be a good thing if the Americans came over to Europe, where he could offer them sport more exciting than mountaineering or skiing. From Denver, he drove to Berthoud Pass and viewed the Rockies. The tree line there rises to 2,000m and the lack of peaks did not impress him. He realised that extensive tree clearance would be needed to open up longer runs.

He went for three weeks to San Francisco and from there visited Mount Lassen, where he suggested setting up a Flying Kilometre such as Walter Amstutz had built at St Moritz. Then he went on to the Midwest, and north to Windsor, Ontario. Wherever he went he continued to write. "And the Floods Came" was published in 1942.

In Boston he lectured to the Appalachian Mountain Club. The lectures were advertised as "Some Experiences of an Honorary Member" and "Can Democracy Survive?", so no one could be accused of British propaganda, but all his efforts went into persuading Americans to side with the British. He thanked them for all they were already doing, especially the

Concord branch of British War Relief, who were providing homes, clothes and education for British evacuees.

He spent Christmas with Hannes Schneider, then went on to the East Coast and Mid-West. Norway had been invaded and he met Oestgaard, who had escaped to Washington. The presidency of FIS had been handed on to Count Hamilton, as Sweden remained neutral. The Nazis had suggested that the next FIS Congress should be held in Budapest, but Hamilton vetoed the suggestion. A FIS race was held in Cortina, but was subsequently not accepted as a World Championship event.

In March 1941 Lunn was present at the annual Far West Kandahar at Yosemite. As he set the slalom with fast open gates to test speed, his mind was on Ernst Gertsch and he regretted that his old friend was not there with him. Then he visited Sun Valley with Hugh Dowding, where they met Averell Harriman, founder of the resort. Friedl Pfeiffer, who had won the A-K in 1936 for the Arlberg Ski Club, and Gerda Paumgarten, who had won the ladies race the same year, were both in Sun Valley. There was a great reunion, including Alice Kiaer, Betty Woolsey, who had captained the American Ladies Team before the war, Rettles de Cosson and many other old friends from past races. The combined ladies event, held during his visit, was won by Gretchen Fraser, whom Lunn described as a dashing and finished skier with superb technique. "She should do well", he prophesied, "in a World Championship". She was indeed to win an Olympic Gold Medal after the war.

Not everything went smoothly. Given a blanket on the chairlift, Lunn caught it under the lift and was dragged off onto the ground, the steel edge of one ski catching his right leg. But as usual he made light of the pain and ignored efforts to get it treated. Lunn played the chess champion of Nevada State at Sun Valley and scored a win and a draw out of four games. The year before he had tied a match with the chess champion of Malta.

After Sun Valley he lectured in the southern states for British War Relief. In Los Angeles he met Aldous Huxley. He was impressed by the hospitality of the Americans, who brushed aside his thanks, saying: "You're our first line of defence, brother". He returned to Britain in a ship that was part of the escort to a convoy.

The lease of their house at Bickley ended in 1942 and Mabel was delighted with the offer of a flat at 127 Victoria Street, very near the church in Ashley Place where her beloved father had been Vicar. "It's so cheap", she said. Arnold was more realistic, pointing out that while bombing continued there was a greater demand for flats and homes in the country than in London. Back in London he found the Ski Club of Great Britain was keeping its clubhouse in Hobart Place open, but with a very reduced staff. The Year Books had a new role. Volumes were used by Mabel and Jacqueta to barricade the windows of their Victoria Street flat against bomb damage, flying glass and shrapnel. As far as possible, Lunn tried to persuade Mabel to stay with her sister in the country while he was away.

Lunn spent the winter of 1941-2 in South America, flying there via the States, where he was besieged by reporters. He told them only that he was there representing the Royal Institute of International Affairs. He found Santiago very European and the Spanish influence was dominant in Lima. He collected photographs of Farellones and La Parva in Chile for the Year Book. The first Kandahar of the Andes was run at Farellones and was a great success, despite thick mist during the downhill, which caused many falls. Even the winner fell about four times.

On a plane from Miami to Washington he met Lord Beaverbrook, whose son, Max Aitken, was a keen skier. skier. Aitken was flying and grateful for the fitness skiing had given him. Lunn was in Washington when the Japanese attacked Pearl Harbour and then he flew home, after a few days in Montreal, via Newfoundland, arriving back on Easter Sunday. Colonel Sturmy Cave was in Washington during the war and Lunn often breakfasted in his rooms.

News reached him of many friends from the skiing world. Digby Raeburn had been awarded an MBE and been promoted to Major. He was at Advance HQ in the desert all winter and his relief was Muffie Mackinnon's husband Murphy. He had gone on leave to the Lebanon, where he met Jimmy Riddell. Riddell was in charge of training troops on the Heights of Lebanon, so that they would be prepared to fight in the mountains. It was strenuous training, which prepared some 20,000 troops of various nationalities. The snowfalls were sometimes so great that they skied straight out of the second-floor windows of their hotel.

Meanwhile, Count Hamilton continued to hold his own for the FIS against the Nazis, and was supported by Aldo Bonacossa. The Nazis suggested that Baron Le Fort should replace Dr Martin of Austria as Chairman of the Downhill-Racing Committee, but Hamilton insisted that Martin, if he resigned, should be replaced by Walter Amstutz.

In the States, a Ski Union of the Americas had been set up to be responsible for the sport on that continent. Roland Palmedo kept Lunn informed. Lunn's only concern was that he might have to edit the next issue of the Year Book from South America, where the post was slow.

PM, an extreme left and very anti-Catholic tabloid, started a tremendous attack on the British Government for sending Lunn to South America. Lunn remained silent, but wrote to Cardinal Hinsley, who was Head of the Catholic Church in Britain. He said Jews were protected, but Catholics were kicked. Robert Speaight, a Catholic author, wrote from the Garrick to the Editor of Reynolds News to defend him. No visitor from these shores, he said, had been a more inspiring ambassador at that difficult time. Speaight had been in America and said Lunn's lecture on the Battle of Britain had electrified the American audience.

In June, Lunn was at 127 Victoria Street, enduring what he called "raidlets". He appeared on the Brains Trust, a thoughtful BBC programme on which C.E.M. Joad was a regular speaker. At this time he was writing "The Good Gorilla", which was published in 1943. It was a blend of religion, politics and scholarship covering the cultures of Greece and Christendom, the Hellenism of Goethe, an Oxford Group house party and Switzerland. He was invited by Sir Hubert Gough to join a few friends to discuss the future of Europe.

He spoke at Cambridge to oppose the motion "The victory for Franco was a disaster for Spain and the World." The mover was an undergraduate, fluent but foolish. He was a communist who prefaced his statements with: "It is generally agreed". Lunn gave exact references for his statements and warned that he would accept none of the mover's unless documented. He won by 54 votes to 41.

"Mountain Jubilee" was also published that year, covering fifty years of climbing and skiing in the Alps. Walter Amstutz provided a magnificent set of photographs to illustrate it. Lunn always felt that this book and "Mountains of Youth" would be the two of all his publications by which he would wish to be judged. In August he was in Spain, where the Infante Alfonso made no secret of his sympathies and helped British pilots who made forced landings to reach Gibraltar. Lunn left for Brazil on 29 September and flew on to Ottawa the following week. In Canada he asked somebody why the Quebec Kandahar was called by that name. "Oh the Cup", came the answer, "was donated by an eminent Britisher, Mr Kandahar." On his journeys he also visited Montreal and Woodstock, Vermont. Murren was playing its part on behalf of the British. Two escaped officers were staying with F.R. Staeger.

Lunn's old friend and climbing companion C. Scott Lindsay who was an active member of the Alpine Ski Club, suggested holding a meeting or dinner during the war. Even during the war Lunn was considering amendments to race rules. He suggested in the British Ski Year Book of 1943 that disqualifications should be posted immediately at the end of a race, so that protests could be heard. He recommended that referees should check with gatekeepers after each run and collect disqualifications. This was later adopted as a rule by the FIS. Lunn gave three lectures at the Ski Club's Hobart Place premises on "Switzerland and the Romantic Revival". In 1944 the Club made him an Honorary Member.

A young American diplomat, George Cooper, came to spend some time during the war in London and happened to stay in the same block of flats as the Lunns. One day Cooper, having just bought a copy of "Now I See" from the Catholic bookshop nearby, put his key by mistake into the Lunn's door. It was a happy accident. Seeing the copy of his book under Cooper's arm, Lunn invited him in. The two men formed a good friendship and Lunn brought both Graham Greene and Robert Speaight to Cooper's flat.

Cooper, later a Professor at Trinity College in Hartford, Connecticut, gave a lecture on Lunn after his death, and intended to write his biography, but sadly his eyesight failed before he could do so.

When the Americans invaded Bavaria, Dr. Karl Roesen produced a letter that Lunn had written to him as evidence that he had always been anti-Nazi. He was immediately given a good job by the American Military Government.

By the end of the war Lunn's mind was focussed on various problems. The definition of an amateur caused him hours of anxiety and covered many reams of paper. He agreed that ski instructors should no longer be classed as amateurs unless the national associations counted them as amateurs – so Swiss were, but Norwegians were not. He printed a proposed set of rules for the FIS in the 1945 Year Book.

He continued to battle against totalitarianism, which his experiences in Germany, Italy and Spain had confirmed, and he also abhorred Russian communism. He did not, however, condemn every individual from a totalitarian country. He instanced Roesen, who had done so much to combat the Nazis. Although the full horror of the Holocaust was not yet revealed, he had heard about Dachau and, while condemning those responsible, he understood how difficult it had been for Germans to fight against such inhumanity while the Nazis were in power. The Year Book contained many pages that were political rather than sporting.

On 25 October 1945 he wrote to Father Martin D'Arcy, a Jesuit friend: "I am just back from Switzerland and have been invited out by the Spanish Government to lecture on skiing in Spain. I had a very entertaining half-hour with the Duke of Alba this morning. He resigned his position as Ambassador when Don Juan issued his manifesto six months ago. Alba was exasperated with Franco, who talked to him about art, about which he knew nothing and the Duke knows a great deal, about history ditto, and gave Alba a little lecture on England. Franco was quite confident of staying where he was because he knew that 90% of the Spaniards did not want another war and he is fairly certain we do not either, and that we do not want Russia at Gibraltar."

Lunn realised that Olympic and World Championship meetings would always attract controversy and zenophobia and regretted the loss of the good spirit of smaller races such as the Anglo-Swiss Universities.

Although news of European resorts was scarce, the Americans kept him informed about developments in their country. In particular he published news of the area near Denver where mountain troops had been trained at Camp Hale. This was to be Vail, which was already stirring into life. News also came from Betty Woolsey, who had settled at a dude ranch near the Grand Tetons in Wyoming. She was enjoying alone what were to become the very popular slopes of Jackson Hole.

In July 1945 he returned at last to Switzerland, with great nostalgia and delight. He called in at the Hotel du Lac in Interlaken to see his old friend Walter Hofmann. He took the train up from Lauterbrunnen to Murren and walked round the upper and lower roads visiting everyone. Then he went on to Zermatt, to help celebrate the 80th anniversary of Whymper's first ascent of the Matterhorn. As he was the sole member of the Alpine Ski Club present, he said he felt able to represent his Club without asking its members.

Phyllis Holt-Needham, his invaluable secretary before the war, had worked for the United Nations during the war and Lunn had news from her occasionally through Mia Woodruff, who worked for the same organisation. Phyllis was in charge of a mixed team of relief workers and Lunn said he should be credited for the ease with which she dealt with awkward people and circumstances. While working for him, he said, she had had plenty of practice.

In September he got permission to visit Italy and set off from Bern to Domodossola, making his way with the help of Army lifts to Stresa, feeling he said a naive astonishment that nothing had changed. At San Remigio he was rowed across Lake Maggiore to be welcomed by the Bonacossas. Phyllis had preceded him and heard how Etta Bonacossa had been called the Mother of the Partisans for the help she had given them.

He received continual correspondence from people who had read "Now I See", and took every opportunity to write back to people to settle their doubts about Christianity. In 1945 "The Third Day" was published. This account of the resurrection of Christ was to convert many waverers.

Back in Switzerland, he managed several visits to Zurich to catch up with his old friend and collaborator Walter Amstutz, who was now an important publisher. Lunn also visited Meiringen, where Max Amstutz, Walter's brother, was Tourist Office Director. He was then invited to lecture on skiing in Spain, where he met Xavier Ribo who was to become a great friend. The two were to exchange letters about mountaineering, skiing, religion and politics. Lunn did not return to Britain until the middle of November. The Year Book was published late, but it completed the war years.

10

1945-49 Back to Racing and Politics

Lunn was proud to find that some of the Year Books he had edited with such care during the war had reached even the cruel Changi Jail in Japan and cheered up the occupants. Field Marshal Montgomery, who was related to Lady Mabel, wrote to say that in the heat of the desert he had looked forward to receiving the Year Book with its welcome pictures of snow and ice.

Lunn continued to be as pro-German and pro-Italian as he was anti-Nazi and anti-Facist. On 23 November 1945 he wrote to Irvine Aitchison, President of the SCGB, protesting that W.R. Rickmers and Count Bonacossa had been taken off the Honorary Members list. He insisted that they should be reinstated.

Rosemary Croxton had taken over as Secretary of the Ski Club of Great Britain, a post she was to hold until 1961. She had a strong influence on the Club throughout those years, and under her control it was to grow and prosper. Scared of no one, she dealt even-handedly with celebrities and unknowns alike. She appreciated the contribution made by Lunn to British skiing and they engaged in friendly controversy combined with mutual respect. Leo Amery said in his President's Report in 1948: "Rosemary

Croxton, concealing a neat little iron hand under a velvet glove, guided me with tact and firmness throughout my tenure of office".

Early in January 1946 Lunn accepted an invitation from the Army Education authorities to lecture on behalf of the War Office in Egypt, Palestine and Syria. He also spent five days in Cyprus, where skiing was being developed by the British. By this time ski-racing had come to mean alpine ski-racing, so the event organised for French, US and British soldiers in Chamonix on 30-31 March consisted of a downhill and slalom.

Einar Bergsland, Vice-President of the Anglo-Norwegian Ski Club, wrote to him from a Norway waking up after the bad dream of German occupation. In February 1946 an international slalom was held at Holmenkollen. Peter Lunn was given special leave to compete by Field Marshal Montgomery. Arnold Lunn was due to leave for a lecture in Singapore, but at the last moment it proved impossible to get a flight, so father and son went to Norway together. It was, of course, a great reunion. The Norwegians managed to overcome the stringencies of post-war life and entertained the British with lavish hospitality. Kandahar members Einar Bergsland, Sigmund Ruud and Rytter Kielland (Secretary of the FIS) met the British in Oslo. Lunn was feted and a dinner was arranged for him with Hamilton, Oestgaard, Irvine Aitchison of the SCGB, Bergsland, Ruud and Peter Lunn, among others. Arnold Lunn reminisced about Baron Le Fort, the German Ski Leader, with whom he had often battled, but without rancour. It was rumoured that the Baron had been killed during the war.

Lunn was not expecting good results from his team, who had had no practice in ski racing for years, but they did reasonably well. Isobel (Soss) Roe, who had been British Ladies Champion before the war, came second Hors Concours. Peter Lunn came 22nd out of 56. In the straight race, Biddy Armitage's time was lost by the wireless in the electric timekeeping. Lunn had already foreseen that this might happen and had specified in his draft of new rules that stopwatches should be used as backups to electrical timing. This was to become a FIS rule soon after.

There was a less important problem for him to worry about too – why had the ladies team been issued with FIS sweaters as if these were World Championships? But when he remonstrated with the ladies, they said happily that Miss Croxton had issued the sweaters, so of course it was quite all right to wear them. And when he remonstrated with Rosemary Croxton, she said that if he felt like that he could, of course, ask the girls to give the sweaters back. Lunn ruefully acknowledged his new status in the Year Book, noting that "Croxton says" has replaced "Lunn says".

The girls treated him with affectionate respect, but occasionally found him maddening, nicknaming him the Sultan. Although so careless about his own clothes, he would complain that they should not wear trousers in the evening. Sheena Mackintosh, following in her family's successful ski-tracks, told of a typical example of absent-mindedness at Arosa, when he put on his evening trousers to go out skiing, got them soaking wet in heavy snow, and so had to wear his ski trousers with dinner jacket and tie at a formal dinner.

Setting the slalom at Holmenkollen, he reflected that the last slalom at which he had officiated had been in California in 1941, and the one before that in Zakopane in 1939. It would be difficult, he thought, for a slalom official to cover greater distances in three successive events.

Lunn was now busy as Chairman of the Downhill-Slalom Committee of the FIS and he was still lecturing. He went to Spain to give a talk to the British Institute in Madrid and Barcelona just before the 1946 edition of the British Ski Year Book went to press. The Review of the Year showed him to be in reflective mood: "I sometimes fancy that the bond which unites skiers is at least as great as that which links mountaineers. We take ourselves perhaps a little less seriously, and consequently our controversies, conducted though they be with great vigour, never attain to the quasi-sacerdotal dignity of the great Alpine Club feuds. Be that as it may, there is certainly no human institution which means as much to me as 'K' and none in which I have so many intimate friends.... I know Murren is not everybody's cup of tea. Murren is in some ways not unlike England. It provokes much the same extremes of affection and distaste."

Lunn was still promoting the use of the Telemark off piste. Tempo turns - tight parallels on rigidly held down bindings - might be fine on the smooth groomed snow of a standard run, but he insisted that the Telemark was essential in heavy snow and breakable crust. For him the beauty of skiing lay in untouched snow, but this was the time when an increasing number of skiers taking short holidays in the mountains were demanding easy conditions – blue runs, groomed snow and the elimination of rocks.

The Ski Club of Great Britain presented him with a set of Alpine prints, as a testimonial after editing the Year Book for 25 years, which he much appreciated.

The Swiss Ladies Ski Club sent an invitation to the British Ladies to race in Zermatt. The SCGB passed it on to Jeannette Kessler and Helen Tomkinson. Helen had four young children and the youngest, David, was only three months old, but her husband Bill encouraged her to go, saying she had been without a holiday for too long. So the two ladies took up the challenge and survived a gruelling giant slalom in Zermatt in spite of being so out of practice. Doreen Elliott and Birnie Duthie were invited to officiate.

The Swiss were immensely hospitable, also inviting the British to St Moritz for a classic Anglo-Swiss race. Hans and Andrea Badrutt opened the Palace Hotel to them. A team was hastily assembled by Robert Readhead, an Army racer, who rang Jimmy Palmer-Tomkinson in Davos, brought Bill Bracken over from Scheidegg as trainer, and arrived with a team of three. Audrey Sale-Barker was there too, as Reuters correspondent.

Marc Hodler, now a lawyer, masterminded a wonderful reunion with all the fun and friendship that had always characterised the Anglo-Swiss races. After his accident in 1938, Hodler he had turned to race organisation, where he was to have an immense influence for many decades. He made a great speech, giving Britain a lot of credit for freeing Europe. The Swiss won convincingly, but the British, seven years older and off skis since they had won in 1939, did not disgrace themselves.

When Mabel Lunn returned to Murren after the war, her health was already failing and, though she continued to help both skiers and bridge players to enjoy themselves, it was a great effort for her. She had stopped skiing, but took an interest in curling and became an enthusiastic supporter of her favourite teams. There were, of course, sad gaps around the big table in the dining room of the Palace Hotel.

The FIS Congress in 1946 was held in Pau and caused Lunn to write 30 turgid pages of rules in the British Ski Year Book. He was intensely political, resenting the power of Russia, even though Russia was not in the FIS (neither, rather surprisingly, was the United States). Lunn forecast that Russia would join and go for skiing in a big way. He wondered how the voting system would work with many countries such as Poland, Lithuania, Estonia, Latvia, Czechoslovakia, Bulgaria, Hungary and even Yugoslavia forming a powerful eastern block. He was, however, wrong in his prediction that the pre-eminence of St Moritz, Sestrieres and Sun Valley would pass to Suvoloffgrad in the Caucasus.

Amateurism again caused a great deal of controversy – Lunn still felt ski instructors should be considered amateurs and that the International Olympic Committee should accept the FIS eligibility rules.

Count Hamilton came to the Congress and Oestgaard was President again. Originally the FIS had not accepted national associations that refused to affiliate clubs for racial or religious reasons – such as excluding Jews. When the Nazis came to power, Lunn had circulated a memorandum to the FIS Council, of which he was a member, reminding them of this rule and saying that it made the Nazi ski organisation ineligible for membership. The only effect of this had been to speed up a rapid change in the rule.

In 1946 communism was the target. A meeting of the SCGB with Leo Amery in the Chair and two ex-Presidents (Kenneth Swan and Malcolm Trustram Eve) present, approved a resolution: "National Associations or National Clubs which discriminate against their own nationals on religious, racial or political grounds shall be ineligible for membership of the FIS." It met with no response. A Russian team turned up to compete in the European Championships in Oslo and was accepted even though Russia was not affiliated to the FIS. Oestgaard, now back in Norway, appealed to Lunn to keep clear of politics.

The World Championships that had been held in Cortina during the war were annulled by the Congress. Lunn spoke of the FIS as a family for the first time. The term was widely used and those who met at congresses and worked together at races did form friendships which made them welcome all over the World.

The Kent rules for citadin racers were also being amended, not for the first or the last time. Eligibility was made stricter, so that those with easy access to the mountains could not qualify. Lunn drafted resolutions about setting up a FIS Calendar and a list of FIS-approved courses, many of which were taken up by the FIS in due course.

Lunn was in the Far East in February 1946, lecturing for the War Office, in Zermatt for three weeks at the end of June, and in Crans in September. In the Year Book that year he nostalgically listed his favourite views: the Wetterhorn from Grindelwald, the Jungfrau from Interlaken, the Matterhorn from Riffelalp, Mont Blanc from the Brevent, the Valaisan Alps from Montana, the Alpine range from Weissenstein, and Maggiore from San Romigio.

In 1947 the joyous return to the mountains continued, thanks to the hospitality of the Alpine and Scandinavian skiers, for Britons were allowed no money for travel. A full calendar of racing was followed, including the Anglo-Swiss University Races. Jimmy Palmer-Tomkinson, who had broken both legs in the war, was commended for winning the downhill after only a couple of days skiing. Nevertheless, the Swiss won again. The Duke of Kent Cup drew racers from towns in Britain, Switzerland, France, Holland and Norway. The Roberts of Kandahar was raced from Scheidegg to Grindelwald and Lunn recalled that the first winner in 1911 had been killed in the First World War, while Geoffrey Appleyard, the last winner of the cup, had been killed in the Second World War.

Lunn was still encouraging the fun element in ski racing and quoted a conversation between Jeannette Oddie (formerly Kessler) with a young French racer who was excited about the magnificent entry of international aces at the Arlberg-Kandahar. A strong French team included many who were to become legends, such as Jean Blanc, James Couttet and Henri

Oreiller. "But the A-K", said Jeannette Oddie, "isn't only a keen competition between experts, it's fun". The young racer paused for a moment and said: "Yes, Couttet tells me that racing was fun once."

The Arlberg-Kandahar took place in Murren, with Lunn setting the downhill. Marc Hodler was praised as Chief of Race by Lunn for setting an excellent slalom. Gratia van den Bergh of Holland, who had raced as Baroness Schimmelpennick van der Oye, championed the cause of the low countries, which she referred to as the "poor flats". At the Copenhagen FIS meeting she, Lunn, Mr Twerp, the President of the Danish Ski Federation, and Roland du Roy de Blicquy of Belgium planned a race for the Danes, Dutch and Belgians. First referred to as the Flatlanders, this became the Lowlander Championships for the four nations.

The first event, which was organised by the British, took place in Murren and was won by the Belgians. The Roberts of Kandahar Cup was awarded for the downhill. Roland du Roy de Blicquy's daughter, Patricia, was a racer and he was to take over the Presidency of the Citadin Committee, which the FIS set up in 1963.

A number of Lunn's rules were accepted by the FIS, including the posting of disqualifications by the Referee immediately after each run of the slalom, with protests to be made within two hours of posting. But he reluctantly gave way over his preference that the same skis should be used by racers for straight and slalom races when competing for the combined. As always, he was striving to make racing follow the natural hazards encountered by a skier coming fast down unprepared mountain slopes. He still felt telemarking to be the fastest method of skiing over ungroomed terrain. He also tried to get the word straight used instead of downhill, because he said that the slalom was also a downhill race - but this was never generally accepted.

Lunn proposed to the FIS that the Chairmen of their technical committees should change every four years. His proposal was not accepted, but he announced that if he were re-elected Chairman of the Downhill & Slalom Committee he would resign in 1950 when his four years were up. He was duly re-elected in 1947, but was not to see through his term.

In 1947 he was writing on several themes. "Is the Catholic Church Anti-Social?", co-authored by Dr G.G. Coulton, and "Switzerland in English Prose and Poetry" were both published that year.

The 1948 British Championships were organised by Ernst Gertsch and Lunn in Wengen, starting on 5 January. Ken Foster wrote an entertaining account for the Year Book, describing how Donald Garrow, who was sent down out of turn, had a conversation with Lunn on the way to winning the combined.

The Oxford and Cambridge Championships started on 11 January and the Flatlanders followed on 14-15 January. The Duke of Kent Cup continued to attract a large and enthusiastic entry. Germany was banned from international sport, but four Britons competed in the Town Teams race from the village of Bad Oeynhausen in Germany.

The Roberts of Kandahar was run in Murren, with the Alpine Ski the day after. Young John Boyagis, who was much later to serve as Chairman and President of the Kandahar, had spent some time in Switzerland during the war, and raced well in the Alpine Ski despite a wrenched ankle. Lunn praised his style.

The Olympics were held in St Moritz. Lunn had walked down the downhill course in the summer and sent a report to the FIS. The racers agreed that it was an excellent and exacting test of skiing at speed. The British Team were benefitting from the opportunity to use Gomme skis. These, the first skis to consist of laminated metal and wood, were made by Donald Gomme of G-Plan furniture, who had been working on the production of Mosquito aircraft during the war. But sadly the British Men's Team were hit by injury: Dodd had flu, Peter Boumphrey dislocated his shoulder, Jimmy Palmer-Tomkinson wrenched his ankle, and Peter Waddell cracked four ribs. Gretchen Fraser, the young American who Lunn had seen race so well at Sun Valley, won the slalom to the surprise of all except Lunn.

Once again, great hospitality was offered by the Swiss. Scheidegg, Wengen and Murren all made generous offers of free accommodation for a limited number of racers, and they did not cancel the arrangement even when a travel ban was announced in Britain and the centres faced a ruinous season. A special allowance was granted by the Treasury for the British Team to compete in the Olympics. But most of the money had to be paid out of the competitor's own funds - the Treasury allowance only covered foreign currency. The Ski Club of Great Britain was still in charge of racing in Britain, but their funds were low as holiday skiing was impossible and the membership could not grow.

After the Olympic Games, Lunn returned to England to debate with Joad. Then he flew back to Geneva, where he was driven to Les Allues in France to see a new resort being developed by Colonel Peter Lindsay. It was to become Meribel, heart of the Three Valleys. Lunn approved of its situation and commented on the convenient teleski, which allowed skiing on one side of the valley while another was proposed for the other side. At that time neither Courchevel nor Val Thorens had been developed.

Then he journeyed on to Chamonix for the Arlberg-Kandahar which, back in 1938, he had promised to hold there when he withdrew from St Anton because Hannes Schneider had been imprisoned. It was agreed that in future the A-K would circulate around St Anton, Murren and Chamonix. The downhill was run on 5 March and the course chosen was the Piste des Glaciers. This had proved so dangerous in 1937 that the World Championship downhill had had to be moved. Fortunately, the course had been improved and was well prepared, but Lunn still described it as 'a desperate affair'. Out of 71 starters, only 41 finished. But the atmosphere of the A-K remained friendly without solemnity, flags or decorations - just 'ferveur et simplicite'.

By this time, Lunn's wide and diverse circle of friends included Albert, King of the Belgians, who was a keen mountaineer, and the Catholic writer Evelyn Waugh. From Chamonix he travelled back to the Bernese Oberland with Godi Michel. In 1948 a new edition of "Mountains of Youth" was published and Hollis & Carter published "Mountains of Memory", another semi-autobiographical book.

In November Lunn enjoyed a day in Ottawa with Mr and Mrs Curle. John Curle was a Diplomat and the first Englishman to compete in the Ottawa Vasaloppet. Lunn then went on to Montreal to see Bruce Carnall at the Red Birds Ski Club - the flag was raised over their clubhouse for the first time. Then he went on to New York, where he was delayed for a week by strikes. The Palmedos and Mrs McAlpine (formerly racer Helen Boughton Leigh) gave him a warm welcome.

As well as continuing to edit the British Ski Year Book for the Ski Club of Great Britain, Lunn was Chairman of the Touring Test Committee and Manager of the British Ski Teams.

The Oxford and Cambridge University races started in Sestriere on 22 December 1948. The Anglo-Swiss University races were, as usual, in St Moritz on 2 January. The British Men's Ski Championships were held in Grindelwald on 6 January, and Lunn was glad to watch Bill Bracken competing against Douglas Mackintosh, the son of his old rival Christopher. The races for the Lady Denman and Lady Mabel Lunn Cups were held in Murren, and the Duke of Kent Cup in the Blumenlucke there on 9 January. The Roberts of Kandahar was raced at Arosa on 14 January, just before the Lowlanders. Douglas Mackintosh emulated his father by winning the race Christopher had won in the early twenties. Lunn announced that this was the World's Senior Challenge Cup for downhill racing.

The 1949 FIS Congress was held in Oslo and was to bring about a major change in Lunn's life. Russia applied for membership of the FIS, coupling their application with three demands. They wanted Russia to be given a seat on the FIS Council, Russian to be accepted as one of the official languages, and the Spanish Ski Association to be expelled from the FIS. Lunn, backed by the Council of the SCGB, voted against Russia's admission. The FIS Council agreed with him that Russians who were candidates for the FIS should not be allowed to move a motion for the expulsion of Spain. This motion was conveyed to the Russians by President Oestgaard. It was ignored. Russia and its satellites, Poland, Bulgaria, Yugoslavia and Romania, spent forty minutes at the Congress attacking Spain. Oestgaard did not call them to order. Lunn said that if the FIS insisted on Russia being elected to the Council after defying them, he would resign. Russia was accepted and with great regret Lunn did resign.

He wrote afterwards that Oestgaard had been in a difficult position because of his appointment at the Norwegian Court. Had he taken a strong line after the Russian delegate ignored the Council's veto on discussion of their Spanish proposal, the communists would have exploited his position at Court to prove that the King of Norway did not want friendly relations with Russia and the monarchy might have been attacked.

Although he had resigned from Council, Lunn expected to remain Chairman of the Downhill & Slalom Committee until the end of his term in 1950, but he was immediately replaced. It was a great setback for him and he was particularly indignant when Oestgaard wrote to Sturmy-Cave of the SCGB saying that Lunn had resigned from Council because he had been replaced as Chairman of the Downhill & Slalom Committee. In a letter to Marc Hodler on 26 May from the Hotel Albana in Weggis, Lunn wrote: "I had resigned from the Council and announced my impending resignation from the Downhill & Slalom Committee some time before I heard that those members of the new Council which met in Oslo, just after most of my friends on that Council had left, had not re-elected me to the Downhill & Slalom Committee." He said he would have been happy to serve on the Committee under the chairmanship of Marc Hodler, if he had stayed on the Council.

Colonel Sturmy Cave, then President of the SCGB, who had gone to Oslo, wrote to Lunn, telling him that Hodler had taken a great deal of trouble to support him. In a letter of 1 June 1949 he wrote about Marc Hodler: "I know he was very indignant. So much so, in fact, that he wasted a whole night to come up to the hotel and see me after he had provisionally left. His affection for you, as well, is most sincere".

On 22 June 1949 Oestgaard wrote to Sturmy Cave saying: "The Downhill & Slalom Committee (8) unanimously voted for Marc Hodler as young man."

There was a sequel from Spain. In a handwritten card of 27 June, Victoria Eugenia, Queen of Spain, thanked Lunn for protesting against the treatment of her country and saying that she was only sorry that it had put an end to his career as a ski politician. Several letters were exchanged between Lunn and Gratia van den Bergh about the Downhill & Slalom Committee.

Despite his anger and disappointment, Lunn wrote to Oestgaard on 20 December saying that it was undesirable that their relations should end badly and, although he did not dislike controversy, he detested quarrels. It was, however, to be ten years before they met again. In support of Lunn, Doreen Elliott resigned from the Ladies Committee of the FIS, and the SCGB, as governing body of the sport in Britain, proposed no replacements.

The three race courses recommended as models for World Championships by the Downhill & Slalom Committee before Lunn left were the Kandahar in Murren, the Olympic in St Moritz and the Piste Verte in Chamonix.

Hugh Kingsmill, the brother with whom Lunn had spent so many happy hours in the mountains as a boy, died in 1949 after a painful illness. He had written several biographies, some novels and criticisms, including book reviews in Punch. His last book was "Progress of a Biographer". Arnold Lunn said of him: "He was better company than anybody I have ever met in a pretty varied experience."

Lunn's correspondence was widespread at this time. Gina, Princess of Liechtenstein, wrote to tell him she was expecting Prince Philip to arrive with Prince Charles and Princess Anne - she was hoping there would not be too much trouble with the Press and that they would have fun. She had seen the Infante Alfonso in Greece and said that he and Lunn were both "full of energy and curiosity like schoolboys and at the same time wise old owls. This seems to me a very good combination". She ended her letter: "I love getting letters from you, they are so perfect (I don't mean the typewriting!)".

A new edition of "Difficulties" was published, with Lunn and Knox both contributing final letters. He acknowledged the help that Knox had given him on his way to his religious conversion.

Son John was proving a problem. He had been mentioned in dispatches and recommended for a medal, but was suffering from the after-effects of war. Lunn wrote to him, saying he must stop spending money and it would be best for him to stay in a home. On Good Friday 1950 Lunn wrote to

Ronald Knox and asked for his prayers for John, who had by then been certified. "The only redeeming fact is that he is not in the least unhappy."

In October that year Lunn visited the Valtournanche. Signor Nasi, who was involved both in Fiat and in Sestriere hotels, drove him from Pallanza to Chatillon, where he caught the bus to Breuil. He stayed in a mountain hut owned by the mountaineer J.A. Carel's grandson, thoroughly enjoying the informality. "I awoke early and as I came out of the Rifugio the alpine turf was still fragrant with the scent of the young hours. I saw the Cervin firm against the clear depths of an October sky and one by one I picked out the famous landmarks, Pic Tyndall, the Grand Tower and Col du Lion." The A-K was held in Sestriere the following year and it joined the regular race circuit.

F.S. Smythe died in 1949 and Lunn contributed an obituary in Lilliput magazine, for which he wrote regularly. Lunn felt he had become mentally unstable, but appreciated that he had been a great climber.

11

1950-56 Very Active in His 60s

In spite of all the drama of 1949, including his resignation from the FIS Council, Lunn wrote a good deal that year. "The Revolt against Reason "was published in 1950 and, now in his sixties, his life continued to be filled with writing, organising ski races, lecturing and constant travel.

At that time there was a great deal of interest in safety bindings because, as currency restrictions were slowly relaxed and holiday skiers multiplied, accidents meant that continental trains carried home increasing numbers of injured holidaymakers. Wavell Wakefield, whose interests had turned from rugby to skiing (he had captained the England Fifteen and took his family to ski in Engelberg), said his daughter Ruth had used safety bindings to win the British Junior Girls Slalom.

Lunn went to Villars for the British Ladies Championships. Villars had an aristocratic British clientele, with its own Villars Visitors Ski Club, headed by Lady Blane, mother of Helen. The Palace Hotel was the centre of activities. Lunn forgot his tie and borrowed one from a page, but it came off during his speech. Fortunately, he was rescued by Hugo Kuranda of The Sunday Times, who provided him with safety pins. He went on to Davos for the Derby, enjoying a very good cocktail party organised by Mrs Hadow, who came from a mountaineering family.

The World Championships were held in Aspen, but lack of foreign currency prevented a full British team from entering. Evie Pinching, whose great run at Innsbruck back in 1936 had won her the World Championship, went out alone to Sun Valley. She was welcomed by the American Girls Team and was trained with them by Friedl Pfeiffer. After 14 years it was a brave try and she earned the respect of the other racers although, as the photograph that appeared in the Year Book shows, she was no longer young. The British Council sponsored Lunn on a lecture tour of Austria, where he met Erwin Mehl, the ski historian and disciple of Zdarsky. Peter Lunn was stationed in Vienna, where he could ski on the Hohe Wand and escape to stay with Major Bracken, who was again in Kitzbuhel.

Lunn wrote that at 61 he enjoyed nothing more than a gentle ski-hike across the Scheidegg to Meiringen at the beginning of March – always a fine month. The Inter-Service Races were in St Moritz, with Lt John Boyagis winning the slalom, downhill and combined. The 1950 A-K was in Murren from 11-12 March. Otto Menardi, who had taken over as Chairman of the Downhill & Slalom Committee, came to Murren and Lunn gave him a list of suggestions to make courses safer for racers. The Germans were represented for the first time since the war. In the spring, Lunn visited Engelberg and enjoyed talking with Adolf Odermatt, whose family were influential in the village.

On 20 August he embarked on a long lecture tour, which lasted until 14 December. He started in Egypt and Pakistan, reaching Australia in September. Tom Mitchell, the Attorney General, made a moving speech congratulating him on publishing the Year Book through the war. In America in October Lunn visited a Trappist Monastery. He wrote a long article on 'Mountains and Metaphysics' for the Year Book, which explains a lot about the way religion and mountains were linked in his mind. He quoted Hilaire Belloc writing about great peaks, which brought him into communion with heaven and ended the article with: "Those physical joys of mountaineering which, though precious, are infinitely less precious than the memory of moments when the mountains were 'lovely with betrayal of divine thought'".

Lord Montgomery wrote a letter to The Times about the decadence of skiing. The Field Marshal approved of skiing offpiste and racing in events like the Inferno, where bravery was tested. He thought the grooming of pistes meant that natural skiing was being abandoned and people were no longer enjoying the wild mountainside. The correspondence grew with many people, including Jimmy Palmer-Tomkinson, joining in, so Lunn reprinted it all in the Year Book. E.C. Richardson recalled the first International Ski Congress, held in 1910, when he maintained: "The international representative is exposed to much the same temptations as the professional".

Lunn visited Val d'Isere for the first time in 1950, but spent quite a lot of his time visiting the Swiss Cantons and collecting material for "The Cradle of Switzerland". He was also preparing "The Story of Skiing", which was to be published the following year. Full of useful information, it was, sadly, also full of inaccuracies. Thereafter Phyllis Holt-Needham did her best to go through his manuscripts and correct them before they were printed. The following year she was also appointed Assistant Editor of The British Ski Year Book.

There was a full month of racing in January 1951, with the British Men's Championships on 4 January in Wengen, the Duchess of Kent Cup two days later in Grindelwald, the Duke of Kent Cup at Scheidegg on 8 January, the Lowlanders in Val d'Isere on 13-14 January, the Lady Mabel Lunn and Alpine Ski in Zermatt on 21-22 January, and the British Ladies Championships on 28-29 January in Klosters. The A-K on 9-11 March was held for the first time in Sestriere.

Arnold Kaech from Bern and Murren, who had won the first Duke of Kent Race in 1938, retired from the Swiss Army and Diplomatic Corps and took over as Secretary of the International Ski Federation. Lunn made a broadcast on Vatican Radio entitled "Rome Through Three Spectacles", about Holy Year in 1950.

In 1952 The British Ski Year Book changed its colour and took on a blue cover. It was no longer, as Alan d'Egville had described it "a little grey tombstone, mostly written in Greek".

Lunn was knighted 'for services to skiing and Anglo-Swiss relations' and on 9 July wrote an enthusiastic letter about the investiture. He hired a suit for the occasion and was amused that he was given a pep talk on how to behave. He practised bowing from the neck rather than bending from from the hips. He said that practically the only people the Queen spoke to - and he thought they certainly deserved it - were policemen decorated for gallantry in Malaya. He was also made a Citoyen d'Honneur by Chamonix. Marc Hodler, elected President of the FIS, came to London to attend the Kandahar Dinner.

At the beginning of October, Lunn flew from Geneva to New York, giving full credit to Swissair when writing about it in the next Year Book. In Geneva he spent a couple of hours with Bonacossa and the French race organisers, Payot and Gignoux, discussing a German request to host the A-K.

During his annual visit to the States, he sandwiched informal talks to various ski clubs between professional lecture engagements. He spent an evening with the Grindelwald Ski Club of Los Angeles and met many friends - Sutter Kunkel, Cortlands Hilland and Clarita Heath among others. He also met Wolfgang Lert, distinguished journalist of Ski Magazine, for the first time. He was driven to see Sun Valley where he regretted that Mount Baldy had been renamed - he preferred the old name, Mount Sant Antonio. He spent a few days in Seattle and then went north to Winnipeg, where he gave a talk to the Puffin Club and stayed with John Curle. He spent two days in Wayzeta near Minneapolis with the Lindley family.

During various visits to New York he was the guest of the Palmedos and said that no kinder hosts could be imagined. "As a guest", Phyllis Holt-Needham remarked, "you must be an acquired taste", but added: "I don't deny that the taste could be acquired."

Lunn lectured to a group of New York skiers and met members of the Council of the New York Ski Club at their Annual Dinner. He spent the weekend at the home of Helen McAlpine. He lectured to the Appalachian Mountain Club in Boston. Then he spent some happy days in Montreal with Sidney Dawes and his wife, who gave a party at which he met Percy

Douglas, the Great Old Man of Canadian skiing. From New York he flew directly to stay in the Gothic Schloss in Vaduz as guest of the Prince and Princess of Liechtenstein.

Also in October, while staying with the Caulfeilds, he wrote to Jeannette Oddie. She was editing the Kandahar Review and had sent him proofs while he was staying in Vaduz. Her husband, Ripley Oddie, had written an article about Lunn and the Princess of Liechtenstein was delighted with his criticism of Lunn's clothes.

Two very different but equally important members of the skiing world died in 1952. One was Jimmy Palmer-Tomkinson, who was killed while race training. As well as being a daring and enthusiastic skier, he was a good organiser and would no doubt have continued to have a good influence on the ski clubs. The other was Alan d'Egville, renowned as a clown who enlivened many parties and whose cartoons and sketches so accurately reflected the importance of having a good time. Lunn was rather indignant that people often asked whether he still skied. "I still ski because I still walk. It is less tiring to slide slowly downhill on ski than to walk along the level."

On 3 February 1953 he was in Murren and skiing. There was a new lift up the Maulerhubel. Coming down from it, Lunn had a bad fall, ending up head down in a hole. Fortunately he was rescued within ten minutes, but he said he had been quite sure he was dying.

The 1953 Arlberg-Kandahar, held in St Anton from 13-15 March, was a cheerful occasion, though the happy-go-lucky organisation rather shocked Digby Raeburn, who wrote the report for the Year Book. Lunn, who was in Davos that weekend, understood:

"The Arlbergers in their heart of hearts feel that the FIS is rather an upstart institution and that the A-K was a great success at a time when the FIS was still dithering about the risks involved in accepting the bold suggestion that a downhill race was a better test of downhill skiing than an uphill one. Hence a touch of light relief was imparted to our otherwise solemn proceedings by dear old Hannes who, in the course of an altercation with Otto Menardi, said that Arnold and he had run the race extremely well before there was any FIS and before it was taken out of our hands, and he added: 'As for the FIS Rules, I spit on them' – which rather appealed to the unregenerate half-Irish part of my make-up".

10,000 spectators watched the slalom. The Prince and Princess of Liechtenstein attended the prize giving and Lunn returned from Davos for a tremendous party. Many great skiers from past A-Ks were there, including Frau Poland, the first winner, Anton Seelos, Sigmund Ruud, Jeannette Oddie, Kini Maillart and Alice Kiaer. Marc Hodler made a good speech. Count Aldo Bonacossa came from Italy and Roland Palmedo from the United States. Ernst Gertsch provided a memorandum of useful and constructive criticism.

The A-K had first circulated between St Anton and Murren, then went to France because of the promise at the outset of the war to go to Chamonix. Sestriere was the venue in 1951. Now Garmisch-Partenkirchen was suggested and a vote taken. Hannes Schneider magnanimously voted for Germany to join, although it was just 15 years since he had been imprisoned by the Nazis.

Lunn took advantage of Sigmund Ruud's visit to discuss the Holmenkollen Kandahar with him. They decided that it would be best to separate the race from the Holmenkollen Week. Lunn spent the Whitsun weekend at the Hotel Marktplatz in Garmisch-Partenkirchen, in order to inspect the new courses for the A-K, which he did not think safe. Dick Durrance, the American ski racer, was there, persuading the Germans to cut down trees to make the course safer. He maintained that a racer who caught an edge might easily be thrown anything from ten to twenty yards.

From Munich, Lunn went to Freiburg in the Black Forest, motoring on Sunday to Feldberg, the cradle of skiing in central Europe, and on to Totdnau. Then he travelled to Berlin, where riots had been suppressed just a few days earlier, and he spent a week with Mr and Mrs Cecil Lyon, whom he had first met in Santiago. From May to July 1953 Lunn was working for the American State Department in Germany. The FIS Congress was held in Innsbruck in May, so he accepted an invitation from Marc Hodler, the new

President, to be the guest of the FIS and of the Austrian Ski Association at their Banquet during the Congress.

Sir Malcolm Trustram Eve, as President of the SCGB, was invited to represent the Club at the FIS Council. At the last moment he was unable to go, so Robert Readhead took his place and was elected to the Council.

It was Marc Hodler's first Congress as President and Lunn admired the speed with which he conducted business and kept people to the point. He felt that the FIS had regained the old "FIS family atmosphere", so noticeably lacking in 1946 and 1949. At the official dinner he made his peace with Andreev, the Russian Delegate. He congratulated him on his election as Vice-President. Andreev responded by coming over with a glass of vodka to drink to Lunn's health.

At that Congress, Gratia van den Bergh resigned her seat on the Council, as did Zaluski of Poland and Moser of Czechoslovakia. The Russian proposals of a Czech and a Pole to replace them were not accepted, but Britain's Robert Readhead, Dr Guy Schmidt of Germany, and Dr Danilo Dougan of Yugoslavia were elected. Helen Tomkinson was elected to the Ladies Committee.

Lunn was in Munich early in June at the time of the Coronation and the first ascent of Everest. He was becoming interested in Moral Rearmament and, as a guest of Robert Readhead's father, made his first visit to Caux, above Montreux, where he spent a weekend at the sect's headquarters, the Mountain House.

After a short visit to Merano for a canoe race named after the Kandahar, he went back to Murren. Sherpa Tensing was there, staying with Ernst Feuz, who arranged for Lunn to meet the hero of Everest.

On 22 August he was in Zermatt with Mabel for the unveiling of a memorial to Frank Smythe. Mrs Smythe recalled that Lunn and her husband had enjoyed corresponding in "tremendous blasts". Long argumentative letters used to arrive in Lunn's own excruciating typing. Apart from some polite remarks to her, Lunn had been so absorbed in carrying on his arguments with her husband that they had hardly ever spoken.

The SCGB was celebrating 50 years since its foundation and Scott Lindsay, who was then President of the Alpine Ski Club, was invited to their Jubilee Dinner. Malcolm Trustram Eve described Sir Arnold as the architect of British Skiing. Hannes Schneider was awarded the Pery Medal. This, the highest SCGB award, commemorates the memory of the Earl of Limerick who, as E.C. Pery, had skied so frequently with Lunn in Murren in the early days.

Avery Brundage was President of the IOC and Lunn said how surprised he was that Brundage still believed it possible to keep the Games amateur. He quoted Godi Michel, who had remarked to him that there was not a single old woman, not even in Africa, who still thinks the Olympic Games are amateur. Lunn and Brundage were to cross swords over amateurism for many years.

In the Year Book Lunn was developing his idea that ski racing should be a test of how fast a skier could get down a mountain. He was very against the "pistification" of racing which, by channelling racers through gates and grooming the slope, meant they were no longer choosing an intelligent line for themselves. A racer's intelligence and mastery of snow-craft should be tested, not only his courage and strength. "Pisting" also cost money. The problem, of course, was that if courses were unpisted, the first few racers left ruts and holes that handicapped those who followed.

So Lunn suggested the Arlom – a long run among the mountains with about five judges provided with score sheets. Marks were to be given for choice of line and control, with fast fluent turns recommended. The highest and lowest marks were to be eliminated. The Arlom was tried out over the years, but the number of judges and need for style marks made it difficult to organise, so it never became popular.

The 31st Roberts of Kandahar Downhill was raced on 5 January 1954 in Engelberg and Lunn enjoyed the atmosphere. The British did well against the other nations, which that year included racers from outside Europe and from Liechtenstein, as well as the Belgians, Danes and Dutch.

In the afternoon, the slalom for the Alpine Ski Trophy was held, with men and women competing down the same course.

Two days later it was the turn of the Anglo-Swiss Races, transferred from St Moritz to Engelberg because snow conditions were difficult in the Engadine. Lunn hoped for good British results as they had already raced the course for the Lowlanders, but he had to admit that the Swiss proved superior and the combined was won by Raul Imseng.

Lunn went to the A-K at Garmisch on 12-14 March. He described the day he came as "one of those March days when the rumour of April fills the mountains with hope and even the lake, in spite of sheets of ice, seemed pregnant with colour. The Bavarian Alps showed through an amethystine haze; among them the old familiar outlines of Altspitze and Zugspitze above Garmisch, and I remembered the smell of mown hay in a field near Garmisch and the full moon rising above the Altspitze in that untroubled summer of 1910".

He had inspected the course in July 1953 and condemned it as unsafe. Garmisch had then spent vast sums blasting rocks and cutting down trees to make it safe. Peter Lunn, Robert Readhead, Digby Raeburn and his sister Patricia, who was Secretary of the Kandahar Ski Club, were all there. Helen Tomkinson represented Elsa Roth, Chairman of the FIS Ladies Committee.

Thanks to the good course preparation and excellent organisation by Garmisch-Partenkirchen, the races went off successfully and the party afterwards lived up to everybody's expectations. A Chilean member of the FIS, Tito Belledonne, attending his first A-K, said he had been to many prize givings, but this was unique - just like a jolly family party.

Lunn was made an Honorary Doctor of Philosophy by the University of Zurich, in recognition of his work for the development and encouragement of Swiss and the Anglosaxon world: "In erkennen seiner Verdienste um die Erforschung und die liebevolle Erlautering Schweizerischer Wesenart fur die angelsachsische Welt". Lunn represented the Ski Club of Great Britain at the Golden Jubilee Dinner of the Swiss Ski Federation in Olten. He also attended the opening of a big new cable car up the Männlichen from Wengen.

He explained the reasoning behind his invention of the slalom, which showed how different it was from the slaloms set earlier by the Austrian technician Zdarsky.

"I regarded ski only as a means to an end, that end being the exploration on ski of the Alps in general and the High Alps in particular. When I turned my mind to ski-racing I was, at first, only interested in competitive skiing as a means for developing the kind of ski technique that would be most useful to a ski-mountaineer. The downhill was an incomplete test, incomplete because it was mainly a test of straight running and it would usually be impossible to include in a downhill course a section of fairly open wood through which skiers could safely be required to race.

I had never seen a slalom and the little that I knew about it did not prejudice me in its favour. The old slalom was a style competition in which competitors had to make particular turns around a mere flag and were marked for style. These slaloms were run on soft snow so that the luck of the draw was usually decisive. On thinking over the matter, it occurred to me that if pairs of flags, i.e. 'gates', were substituted for single flags and marks for style were eliminated and time was the decisive factor, the slalom might be turned into a kind of gate race which would test every variety of turn, long and sweeping, short and abrupt. Suppose the first run were on hard snow, the second on soft. Suppose further that the order in which the competitors finished in the first part determined the order in which they started for the soft snow part, the privilege of racing down comparatively untracked snow would be the reward of victory in the hard-snow slalom and not the draw."

Lunn had given up setting slaloms after the war but went back to doing so for the Lowlander races. He was determined to keep the slalom as a natural race through trees, where a racer did not have a track to follow, but made his own mind up about where to turn. "Let us remember that when we find ourselves at the top of a wood glade we cannot say: This is unfair. If I take this too fast I shall fall. I'm going to take off my ski and walk home."

He deliberately left enough space between gates for racers to have to turn. Judging where to turn sorted out the best racers. For a third time, Lunn referred to the finish of the Roberts of Kandahar race in 1931, when Jimmy Riddell fell towards the end because there was no Finish banner.

He praised the beauty of Stein Eriksen's skiing: "I have seldom in sport seen anything lovelier than Stein Eriksen when he is slaloming at the top of his inspired form." The Norwegian had won Gold at the 1952 Olympics. Lunn foresaw the day in the future when wax or the curve of the ski or a different arch and slightly different edges would make the difference between winning or losing a race.

There was a suggestion that downhill races for ladies should be abandoned in favour of giant slaloms. Lunn thought this quite wrong and he supported the Ladies Committee, who wanted to continue racing downhill.

He never forgot his classical education and was often teased about the amount of Greek and Latin he used in his publications. In 1954 he wrote to The Times in a rage because the Greek inscription on Olympic medals had been supplanted by a Roman one – Citius, Altius, Fortius. This led to a lively exchange of letters – many addressed from Oxford or Cambridge – which he reprinted in the Year Book. Fortunately, the invaluable Colonel Bowdler, also with a classical education, was still reading the proofs. Lunn thanked him and also thanked Phyllis Holt-Needham, who made sure all the pages were in place.

In reviewing a book called "High Mountains" by C. Meade, Lunn gave his own reasons for behaviour. "A gentleman recognises certain obligations, i.e. to volunteer at the outbreak of war and not to cheat at cards, etc., but where his code comes into conflict with the Christian code it is the latter which is ignored. The Catholic Church, for instance, forbade duelling and declared that those who died in a duel died in a state of mortal sin. But men of honour continued to fight duels".

Meanwhile he continued his opposition to "shamateurism", mostly against the Russians whom he considered full-time paid athletes. He argued that money intended for those whose work was interrupted by training should not be paid to Russians whose job was ski-racing.

Always ready to repeat criticism of himself, especially if it made a good story, Lunn printed a race report that said he did not watch while gatekeeping. He disarmingly agreed in the Review of the Year that: "My attention sometimes wanders in races, which is why the authorities are reluctant to entrust me with the responsible duties of flag-keeping."

At some time in 1954 Lunn was invited to travel on the maiden voyage of the "Olympia" to New York. Lord Donegall, Toby O'Brien and Lord Keyes, all friends of the Kandahar or SCGB, sailed at the same time. He spent four days with Roland and Betsy Palmedo, arriving on the evening of a joint ball held by all the ski clubs of New York.

Lunn watched the Inferno on 29 January 1955 with Field Marshal Montgomery. It was just three years since the Montgomery Cup had first been awarded for teams of 4 schoolboys in the Lauterbrunnen region.

Lunn had written "Zermatt and the Valais" and suggested to Phyllis Holt-Needham that, in return for indexing his book, she should visit Zermatt for the Gornergrat Derby. She did so, met the Bonacossas there and wrote a charming piece for the Year Book about her visit.

Lunn made a last ascent at Chamonix, but suffered a good deal while doing so. He also had a severe ear infection in the last stages of preparing the Year Book, so Phyllis Holt-Needham came to the rescue and finished it.

The 1955 Year Book covered the usual wide range of subjects. It told how to build an igloo, described skiing in the Lake District and Scotland as well as tours in the Alps; Kaspar von Almen of Kleine Scheidegg wrote despairingly of amateurism; Christian Rubi, Head of the Swiss Ski School, wrote about teaching; and Helen Tomkinson covered the Swiss Ladies Ski Club races in Grindelwald, where Lunn made one of his famous speeches in three languages.

There were two notable deaths that year. Hannes Schneider had a heart attack and died in New Hampshire. Lunn wrote a moving obituary for the great Austrian. He had had an immense influence on the spirit and the prestige of the Arlberg-Kandahar. Before the war, he had always been on the platform to greet Lunn and great celebrations had marked his return to St Anton in 1949 and 1953. General Ivar Holmquist, who had been President of the FIS for its first ten years, also died.

Lunn went to Val d'Isere at the beginning of the season to represent the Kandahar at the Roberts of Kandahar and he stayed with the team in the Christiania Hotel. He also went to Cortina for the 1956 Olympics, as guest of the town, and stayed at the Tre Croci Hotel, owned by Otto Menardi, Chairman of the FIS Downhill-Slalom Committee. The Russians were staying there too, and he admitted to a momentary discomfort every time he saw the Soviet flag flying overhead. Rather wryly he concluded that Olympic medals would eventually become the monopoly of those countries that pay the biggest salaries to their amateurs.

He left Murren on 10 May after giving rise to another story about putting on a tie given to him as an Honorary Member of the Army Ski Association and then adding a FIS tie. He wrote a good deal about the pleasures of controversy.

Karl Weber was the President of the Swiss Foundation for Alpine Research and was to support Lunn for many years, subsidising publications for which he wrote, providing an apartment in Murren when the Palace Hotel was taken over, and often arranging for a taxi to transport the Lunns from Stechelberg to races.

Gerald Seligman reported in the Year Book on an avalanche below the Ulmerhutte, which caused the deaths of six people, four of them British. He took the opportunity to draw some useful lessons from the tragedy and recommend that the SCGB should include more about snow lore for its members.

Otto Menardi wrote an article on the giant slalom for the Year Book and Lunn added his own comments. Lunn was still hankering after the slalom testing the speed of a skier down mountain slopes and the choice of where to turn. He scorned what he called ballet-dancing on skis. Roland Palmedo organised a race at Mad River Glen called the New England Kandahar.

The Arlberg-Kandahar opened at Sestriere on 9 March. Lunn went to it after a couple of days with the Sella family in Biella. Peter Lunn refereed the downhill. They held a Requiem Mass for Hannes Schneider on the Thursday before the race. Arnold was lecturing to a priest's seminary in Sion ten days later and was amused to be introduced as the man seen kissing the winner when awarding a prize.

He continued to inveigh against false amateurism, insisting that countries under the power of communism, such as Russia and Czechoslovakia, paid their athletes in secret, either by giving them spurious jobs or awarding them money prizes. He felt keenly the fact that the British were no longer winning, nor even losing gracefully. He felt Britain should cut out amateurs and professionals and just have players. He recommended forming a Ministry of Sport, putting all training and coaching on a nationally organised basis, building new and properly equipped stadia and making sure all youngsters who showed real talent were given the time, facilities and financial aid they needed to reach world class.

Lunn wanted to climb Mont Blanc, which he had never done, but he knew Mabel would worry about him climbing. In July 1956 Mabel was in England for the wedding of a nephew. Lunn went to Murren for a week and composed five reasonably convincing letters to be posted to her while he went off to Chamonix. They were carefully worded to convince her that he was writing a book in Murren. With Camille Tournier, a famous guide, he climbed 1,500m to a hut on the Tete Rousse. He confessed that five hours of climbing was all he could manage. Then the weather broke and after a try the next day, the attempt had to be abandoned.

The Press, however, had learnt about the failed attempt. So on the same day that Mabel read in the papers that bad weather had prevented his climb, she received by post a letter complaining that life was dull in Murren, but he was getting on well with his writing. It was to be some years before he finally stood on the summit.

12

1957-61 Enjoying Good Arguments

There were great celebrations in Zermatt for the Centenary of the Alpine Club. About 80 members attended, including Sir John Hunt. Lunn had been commissioned by the Swiss Foundation for Alpine Research to write "A Century of Mountaineering". Reckoned to be one of his best books, it covers the golden age of mountaineering and combines a practical and a philosophical love of the mountains. It shows Lunn's classical education and great descriptive powers.

He described the village of Zermatt, which he had visited first in 1908, before it began to attract winter visitors. The local people had then lived on goat's meat, milk and cheese, and skis were unknown. In the book, he quotes his definition of sport as the invention of an artificial problem for the fun of solving it.

The 1957 Arlberg-Kandahar was in Chamonix. Sadly, Mabel Lunn was ill in St John & St Elizabeth Hospital, where Phyllis Holt-Needham visited her before leaving London and brought her good wishes for the race. Phyllis wrote a good account of the background to the race.

The Alpine Ski Club, too, was looking forward to celebrating an Anniversary - its 50th - in 1958 and Scott Lindsay reminisced in the Year Book about its foundation, borrowing a term from the stud book to say that the club was "by Arnold Lunn out of Protest".

As well as a new edition of "The Bernese Oberland", Lunn had published that year "Enigma" and "And Yet So New". The first was about Moral Rearmament, written from a Catholic point of view. Lunn had learnt a good deal about this philosophy and felt it was misunderstood by most Catholics. "And Yet So New" was a description of Catholicism written by a Catholic, with anecdotes from his own life.

A major article promoted Lunn's idea that slalom poles should be topped with a cup into which was placed a ball. If the ball was knocked out by a racer, it meant disqualification. The aim was to make racers turn accurately and to prevent slalom poles being knocked down. Lunn was sure it would reduce the need for many gatekeepers – or flagkeepers as they were still called. He felt it brought the slalom back to his original idea of a test of skiing through trees – you cannot push a tree aside on your way down. It would also save the time allowed for racers to protest against disqualification, which in those days was two hours.

This theory obsessed Lunn for many years and his friends grew tired of his constant arguments. When Marc Hodler came back to his chalet in Murren and knew Lunn was in the village, he would walk along the lower road to avoid the watchful figure waiting to catch him and argue. Arnold Kaech was another of those living Murren who tried to escape being kept standing for long discussions in the cold.

But Lunn continued to argue with his friends and in the Year Book about the failure to enforce amateur rules. He felt countries did not stop their own racers taking money because "unfortunately the commercial value of racing successes for a country competing for skiing tourists is too great to indulge in any amateur idealism."

When the Russians brutally suppressed a Hungarian revolt in 1957, Lunn applauded initiatives all over the World from sportsmen refusing to compete with Russians. He visited Scheidegg soon after Easter. Skiing conditions that year remained good right up to 10 June.

At the end of June he spent a weekend in the Albergo Golf at Magliaso, near Lugano, which belonged to the Borter family, who also owned the Palace Hotel in Wengen. Then, after attending the Annual Congress of the Swiss

Ski Association in Champex, he was driven back to Lauterbrunnen with Ernst Gertsch and Karl Molitor. Both were very involved with ski equipment. Gertsch had invented a useful safety binding, while Molitor was famous for his ski boots. Naturally, they were all very much in favour of safety bindings. Godi Michel, who had recently been re-elected as President of the Swiss Ski Association, was encouraging all ski shops to fit them to hired skis. There was some opposition from ski instructors as they took time to put on, and in beginners classes they tended to cause delays when they worked loose.

The Year Book was full of practical advice. Doreen Elliott wrote a piece for beginners on snow conditions Lottie Warburg, who ran Harrods' ski department, wrote about choosing ski boots, and further articles described new equipment and skiing round the World, and there were book reviews and obituaries. The Ski Club of Great Britain awarded its Pery Medal that year to Count Aldo Bonacossa.

When his typing was criticised for being unreadable, Lunn advised: "If ever a word puzzles you, take a typewriter and try the next letter to the one which puzzles you". He was apt, in his haste, to put his fingers on the wrong keys.

Lunn was sent news of the FIS Congress in Dubrovnik and regretted the resignation of Otto Menardi from the Downhill & Slalom Committee. However, he was glad that Friedl Wolfgang, who had raced in the A-K before the war, had taken his place.

The Ski Club of Great Britain awarded Honorary Membership to the Shah of Persia and asked Lunn to present the badge. He had also been invited by the British Council to make a lecture tour in the Near East on skiing. This included a week in Teheran, so the two coincided very conveniently.

The journey started with a flight from Geneva to Beirut and Lunn enjoyed the view of the mountains as the Swissair plane flew across the Bernese Oberland, over the Wetterhorn and Lake Lucern. His memories aroused, he wrote some great prose:

"From the plane I could pick out that little terrace where my friends and I had idled away a perfect afternoon. The Dollfuss shelf was still there, far below, cold and pale and ghostly as if the colours of spring had been drained away when the voices of my friends had been stilled by death. Those peaks shimmering in the faint moonlight were not the peaks I had loved and climbed, but phantom mountains as unsubstantial as the phantoms of past happiness which they evoked. I was glad when we left the Oberland and glided over less-haunted snows towards the plain of Piedmont."

But his self-deprecating sense of the ridiculous remained. He also remembered that he had been in Beirut in 1913, guiding a party for his father. On that occasion one of his charges had been unkind enough to remark to the Managing Director on return: "Well, we've brought back your conductor safely."

On a previous visit the authorities had organised for him to visit the Cedars of Lebanon, but he had revised the schedule so that he could visit Jerusalem, Bethlehem and Nazareth instead. Now he was fascinated by the many religions in the city and felt his father would have been delighted to see such an ecumenical crowd.

From Beirut he went to Teheran, where he had the usual problems with his clothes. Lady Mabel, ill in England, had not been able to pack for him. His friends in Murren had checked that he looked suitably clad and for once he had not had to return from Lauterbrunnen because he was wearing one ski boot and one town boot, as had happened in the past. He had, however, failed to pack his evening shoes. Fortunately, Rosemary Croxton (by then married to Stephen Tennant), Secretary of the SCGB, came to the rescue and managed to send them to Teheran in the Diplomatic Bag.

Only once in the Peacock Palace did he have to be reminded to put on a tie. He was well entertained on his way by Ambassadors and Ministers, and appreciated the honour of lunching with The Shah and the Queen in the Shah's suite. He took a lot of trouble over the speech, in which he said he did not ration flattery. The Shah was an outstanding athlete and a very good skier. A letter from Sir Roger Stevens at the British Embassy said afterwards: "The Shah was delighted with 'the unusual honour' by an unusual person".

Although he much enjoyed the visit, Lunn admitted afterwards that it had been quite a strain, with endless parties and the need to be constantly polite and attentive to important Persians. But he felt the effort was worth making because the trip was costing the Government over £400.

He flew from Beirut to Athens and lectured for the British Council on mountains and skiing. Athens, where John Curle was then Ambassador, awoke his classical dreams. Officials and about a hundred members of the Greek mountaineering and skiing clubs drove some ten miles to a mountain hut on Mount Parnis to entertain him at a special party. Lunn then went on to Ankara to lecture to the Istanbul Mountaineering Club, before returning home to lecture in the University Church in Cambridge. The Cambridge University Ski Club and Climbers Club entertained him to dinner.

He returned to Murren for a few days before leaving for the A-K at St Anton, which took place on 7-9 March. Though Hannes Schneider was sadly missed, his daughter Herta was there to present the prizes. Tony Sailer was vorlaufing, Christian Pravda raced and Karl Schranz won the A-K for the first of many times. Past champions, ex-racers and tourist directors including Frau Poland, Walter Amstutz, Fred Ruby of Adelboden, Werner Grob of Arosa, and of course Godi Michel were there to watch. It was, as always, a great race with a great party atmosphere.

Lunn, not surprisingly after a hectic schedule during the previous couple of months, was feeling his age and afterwards wrote:

"The prize giving at St Anton was in the open air, so all the village could attend. I walked along to the prize giving feeling that I would speak briefly and formally. 30 years ago I was only a generation from the racers. I knew most of them and the kind of lighthearted speech in four languages became a tradition. Odd how, even now, people come up and say how they laughed over something I said many years ago. Now I feel out of rapport and that some young racers will say: 'Who is that funny old man?'

So I decided to be short and solemn, but I met Peter on the way, who made some amusing comments about the Austrian police, who expressed regret when they had to turn people back and extreme regret – ausserordentlich wei – when they had to turn back a pretty girl, and I immediately saw that this was the kind of simple theme that could be built up for that kind of audience, particularly in the open air. Austrians are tremendously quick on the uptake and they gave a delighted yell at my first little joke and then, of course, I thought of others as I went along. Arlbergers kept coming up and saying they had laughed til they cried. What puzzles me, seeing how easy it is to make people laugh and what elementary jokes do the trick, is why the overwhelming majority of speeches on these occasions are so humourless."

He was, however, indignant that when he climbed onto the podium to give his speech Ernst Skaderasy of Zurs tied a rope round him. "This was too much, to be roped for the descent of a ladder. After all, I was a mountaineer – once".

In St Anton, the date for the following year's A-K was discussed and Lunn thanked Ernst Gertsch for his support in scheduling the Lauberhorn earlier than usual so that the A-K did not clash with the Squaw Valley Olympics. Gertsch might have withdrawn support, for it did not help the Lauberhorn.

Meanwhile Karl Erb, son of Lunn's old friend Fritz Erb, was writing in "Sport" about the A-K as the chief event of the following winter. Lunn left, resolving to survive at least two more A-Ks in St Anton and full of nostalgia for the days with Hannes Schneider.

He was due to travel next to Oslo to make a presentation on behalf of the SCGB to the Ski- Idrettens Freme (society for the promotion of skiing), which was celebrating its 70th Anniversary, and the Norwegian Ski Federation, which was celebrating its 50th Anniversary. Jakob Vaage, the Norwegian ski historian, had said he would very much like to have an evening with Lunn to discuss the slalom. Einar Bergsland had arranged a full programme.

He was worried about Mabel, who was not well, and he had fallen out with Montgomery, who eventually handed over the Presidency of the Kandahar Ski Club to the Earl of Selkirk in the autumn. Lunn was also suffering from sinus trouble and a stomach upset. So he wrote to Rosemary Tennant in March 1958, saying that he didn't really want to stay a whole week in Oslo, where he might have to sit out in the cold and watch the jumping. He agreed, though, that if it would cost the SCGB more to bring him home early he would stay there, and he signed the letter: "Your dutiful and obedient Council Representative." If he had to go, he felt it would be polite to call on the Embassy, which was far from where he was to stay, so he also asked Rosemary Tennant to write in advance and say he would be visiting Oslo on behalf of the SCGB. They might, he suggested, even send an Embassy car for him. Ill or not, he did go, travelling with the Austrian Team to Oslo. It was a lively journey with pillows flying in the plane.

Einar Bergsland welcomed Lunn to Oslo and said that Oestgaard was in hospital. So Lunn went to visit his old friend and adversary. It was the first time they had met since Oestgaard, as President of the FIS, had let the Russians attack the Spaniards and turn them out of the organisation, which caused Lunn to resign. Lunn was determined to heal the rift between them and he did so. They talked about the FIS, which Bonacossa had just left – the last of the old guard.

It had been in St Moritz in 1928 that Lunn and Oestgaard, together with Hamilton, had laid the foundation of enduring friendships. It had been Oestgaard who had reproached Lunn with the words: "What would you think, Mr Lunn, if we Norwegians tried to change the rules of cricket?" But it was also he who, after his visit to Murren in 1931, wrote in defence of downhill racing and told Norwegians the time had come for their criticisms of Alpine races to stop. Oestgaard was to die the following year.

Lunn was, in fact, sad when the time came to leave Oslo, but he had had a long and exhausting journey since leaving Murren. He wrote to Phyllis Holt-Needham saying that he was suffering from 'fatigue du Nord'. He admired Norway as the country where amateurism is most strictly observed, but Oslo was cold and grey whereas Primavera was scattering her flowers on the meadows of Maggiore.

While in Oslo, although tired, he found time to write a paper on the A-K. "I claimed after the war the right for the Kandahar to nominate the Chairman of the A-K Committee, but I have gradually been coming to the opinion that we should not claim a privileged position. The main thing from the point of view of British skiing prestige is to keep the A-K at the top and secure the real cooperation of the other Alpine countries". Godi Michel said: "The K got this because in the old days they were essential for organising this race before the Alpine countries learned how to run alpine races".

Lunn celebrated his 70th birthday at the Hotel du Lac in Interlaken, and lunched at the Trummelbach with the von Almens and Othmar Gurtner. He was called to the telephone in the middle of the meal. After an animated discussion on a skiing controversy, forgetting the birthday party, he returned to the solitary table at which he normally sat. As the headwaiter approached he looked thoughtfully at the menus. "You've had the first two courses", said the headwaiter, "at another table. Perhaps you would like to finish your meal there?"

As a 70th birthday present, the Swiss Foundation for Alpine Research arranged a flight with Hermann Geiger, a great mountain pilot, from Sion to a point near the summit of the Tete de Valpelline. He looked forward eagerly to the whole trip as offering a fantastic view from the plane over the mountains he had explored as a boy above Montana with his brother Hugh and the ascent of the Wildstrubel he had achieved in 1908.

It lived up to his expectations and turned out to be one of the happiest days of his life, in spite of the considerable effort involved. With Walter von Allmen from Murren and Hans Furrer as guides, he climbed to the summit. The day ended with about 1,525m of varied skiing down to Zermatt. It was, he said, 'like coming home' and the ski down rejuvenated him. "I have learned to distinguish between the Architect and his creation, but I often wonder in what desert of scepticism I should still be wandering but for the revelation of God in the temporal loveliness of the mountains."

Bob Handley wrote an article for the Year Book about the achievements of the Alpine Ski Club. Foreign members included the great continental pioneers Paulcke, Rickmers, Roget, Kurz and Bonacossa. Its members had pioneered the great glacier ski tours, helped to develop skiing in New Zealand, established a height record on Kamet (R.L. Holdsworth in 1931) and made the first ski crossing of the Coast Range in British Columbia

(Bentley Beauman and Norman Watson in 1934). In the same year Frank Smythe climbed the 7,000m Ramthang Peak in the Himalayas, and in 1950 and l951 Colin Wyatt explored the Atlas mountains.

The Alpine Ski Club's literary successes had started with Arnold Lunn's Alpine Ski Guide to the Bernese Oberland and included "Alpine Skiing at all Heights and Seasons", as well as Gerald Seligman's "Snow Structure and Ski Fields" and many other contributions to alpine literature.

Many of Lunn's friends died in 1958, including Vivian Caulfeild, with whom he had discussed ski technique so thoroughly. An article appeared the following year in "Skiing", the American ski magazine, and Lunn wrote to the Editor. He said that Tony Sailer was not the only person to develop ski technique. Zdarski had described stem turns with short skis and a single diskless pole. In 1911 Caulfeild had published "How to Ski", the first clear analysis of ski dynamics and the first book to denounce stick riding. Major Bracken died in Wales on 8 January. The father of Britain's great racer, Bill Bracken, it had been his invitation to Kitzbuhel that had led to Lunn meeting Hannes Schneider back in 1927.

Another death was that of Geoffrey Winthrop Young, who had been Best Man at Arnold's wedding. A mountaineer and poet, he had lost a leg above the knee in 1917 when commanding a Friends Ambulance Unit. He continued to climb after having a special artificial leg fitted for climbing rocks. A sort of steel pencil with the point sharpened gave him a sure foothold on any pitch.

Lunn's reports to the SCGB Council emphasised the need for more money if British ski racing was to have any future. There was no hope of getting money if funds were wasted on entering racers for events in which they were hopelessly outclassed.

The slalom-pole innovation was tried out for the Lady Mabel Lunn Challenge Cup in Murren on 24 January 1959. This time, knobs were put on top of slalom poles instead of tennis balls, but they were not a success as they were less sensitive and did not always fall out when they should have.

The A-K, held in Garmisch from 6-8 February, was marred by the death of a young Canadian racer, John Semmelink, who plunged off line and through bushes, hitting his head. No blame was put on the organisers, but Lunn spent much time looking for lessons that would prevent such an accident from happening in future. He recommended again that downhill courses should be inspected by FIS representatives in summer, so that the ground on which the snow lay could be assessed.

After the A-K, Lunn spent a few days in Kitzbuhel where the Alpine Ski Challenge Cup took place. He suggested a new race, the Methuselah Cup, for those who had begun to ski in the last century, to be awarded on the result of a 'dwarf (not giant) slalom'.

Lady Mabel was ill in hospital, so Lunn went back to Britain to see her. She returned home to the flat in Victoria, but had a relapse into depression. She would not go out to Murren and did not want Jacqueta brought back from Amman, where she was working. She and Arnold corresponded constantly and she assured him she was quite recovered.

A letter dated 18 February said: "I am so happy it is not true. Sir Daniel has given me a clean bill of health, but told me to go slow at present, which I do…I am not letting the flat. It will do for us both for many years to come. You will be able to stay here when you come back in the spring."

Lunn went to Engelberg in the last week of February for the Swiss Championships meeting. It was at the World Championships there in 1938 that Hannes Schneider had announced to a group of friends that Austria would never be German. A fortnight later the Anschluss had been carried through and Hannes was in prison.

On 4 March 1959 Lady Mabel died. Walter Amstutz printed a booklet compiled from tributes by her friends. Before the war she had been a skilful and brave skier, but a leg injury had prevented her from skiing for some time and her doctor had advised her not to go out to Murren. The funeral was held in her Parish Church of St Stephen's and a Memorial Service was also held in Murren's English Church.

Lunn was awarded the Order of the Gran Cruz d'Isabel la Catolica by the Spanish. A reviewer in The Times Literary Supplement gave him credit for "controversy conducted with wit, gusto, good humour and with that strong masculine trust in words and disregard for ambience which makes the best debates. To Sir Arnold argument is an intellectual joy, a skilled exercise, a sword dance which demands an opponent partner."

Lunn himself praised James Hutchings of the Year Book's printers, King & Hutchings, acknowledging that he wrote much of his contributions on the back of race results and old correspondence, a practice that could create difficulties. Hutchings once wrote to Rosemary Tennant: "I always take the precaution of glancing at the back of the pages on which Mr Lunn writes his articles and have thought it best to return to you a letter from the Income Tax Collector to Lady Mabel Lunn. I have had the page of Mr Lunn's article on the back of his letter retyped by a confidential secretary." Lunn also acknowledged the help of Phyllis Holt-Needham, remarking that he often saw the letters pwb - meaning please write better - on his manuscripts.

At the end of the season in Murren, Lunn spent a week at Melchsee Frutt above Saanen, which he had first visited when writing "The Cradle of Switzerland". Then he went on to Scheidegg where he always spent his birthdays. Leaving Murren again on 15 May, he found enough snow to ski to the bottom of Shrub Slope on the Halfway House run. J.A. Joannides was at Scheidegg and they discussed whether the race at Garmisch, when Semmelink died, should have been stopped.

On 9 June 1958 he was on his way to stay with Countess Lippens in Belgium, and wrote to Douglas Woodruff of The Tablet saying that he saw a great deal of the Queen of the Belgians during the years she came to Murren. He and Mabel had stayed at Laaken, her Palace. She was, however, known as the red queen because of her sympathy with the Soviets.

Lunn celebrated the 50th Anniversary of the Oxford Mountaineering Club in May – but remembered just before the Dinner that he had spent the summer term of 1909 in London, after being sent down from Oxford. No Minute Books of the Club had survived, but it was more likely that he had founded it in the summer term of 1908.

He never tried to hide his absentmindedness. On 20 May he wrote a characteristic card to Rosemary Tennant: "I wrote to you today and can't find the postcard. I may have posted it. It was to say that my address after

Thursday is c/o HSH The Princess of Liechtenstein". He also spent a pleasant week in May in Biella, with the Sella family. Vittorio Sella had been a well-known mountaineer and his brother Quintino pioneered mountain photography, taking a great box camera and tripod up mountains with him. Mrs Sella was the daughter of Lunn's great friends the Bonacossas. He enjoyed the week, complaining only at the way music was now played on chairlifts. To him, the silence of the mountains was more beautiful than any music.

Godi Michel, now President of the Swiss Ski Federation, paid a compliment to the British Ski Year Book at their Annual General Meeting. He was urging the Swiss to continue publishing their magazine "Ski", and said that all prominent European skiers who were able to read English read and referred to the Year Book.

Lunn went to Stockholm to attend the FIS Congress. Sigge Bergman, Secretary of the FIS, gave him a great welcome and presented him with the FIS Portfolio as if he had been a FIS Delegate. Friedl Wolfgang, as Chairman, invited him to attend the Downhill Slalom Committee. Einar Bergsland (calling him Uncle Arni) commended his new rule for "unseen" slaloms, but Lunn lamented that not one member of the Downhill Slalom Committee had tried out his ball-pole slalom. He insisted that the FIS needed a definite procedure for testing any innovation suggested by men whose judgement they respected.

He proposed some changes to the FIS. He agreed that the Executive Committee consisting of the President and three Vice-Presidents, representing the Alpine countries, Scandinavia, the American continent and the Communist Bloc, was fair, but that the American continent should not be represented on all committees by citizens of the USA. He argued that it was quite wrong for the whole Spanish-speaking world to be excluded from the Council.

He also thought that there should always be at least one lady on the Council. The FIS, influenced perhaps by its Swiss base, was notoriously unwelcoming to lady members. Only Gratia van den Bergh had managed to penetrate the male sanctum of the Council in the early days. Lunn suggested that the President of the FIS Ladies Committee might perhaps be an ex-officio member without the right to vote, unless she was also the only representative of her country, but this was not accepted. Both Count Hamilton and Count Aldo Bonacossa were in Stockholm – Bonacossa was very impressed by Marc Hodler's skill as President. For several years Lunn put a running joke in the Year Book, trying to persuade Marc Hodler to write an article.

At the end of 1959 Lunn was invited to give the Lowell lectures in Boston – the blue ribbon of American lecturing. His theme was the general influence of sport on society, beginning with the classical Olympic Games. Modern illustrations were based on his own experiences in skiing. His main conclusion was that in sport, as in many more important matters, we had failed to cope successfully with totalitarian regimes because we would not admit that Nazis and Communists simply ignore the codes we profess.

He flew from Zurich to the States by Swissair. Absent-mindedly, he failed to fill in an entry form, but the official at Immigration filled it in for him. When asked the reason for his visit, he replied that it was to give the Lowell Lecture and the official said: "You must be very learned". They had a chat about Jack Kennedy's chances of being elected President of the USA, and the official remarked: "I ought to have sent you back to fill in your form properly, but I said to myself this guy's conversation will be worth the trouble." Lunn, thinking of Phyllis Holt-Needham's apt criticisms, wondered if his former Assistant Editor would agree.

After spending a few days in New York with Roland Palmedo, he spent a week with the Hartford Ski Club. Cardinal Cushing of Boston was encouraging about his interest in Moral Rearmament, saying that they were "dedicated people, self-sacrificing, most edifying and, in very truth, they put us to shame".

The 1960 racing season started with the Men's Championships held, with the Juniors, in St Moritz from 5-10 January, with the Aga Khan competing. Lunn went to Davos for a Ladies Ski Week, organised by Mardens, from 19-24 January. He commended those ski instructors who took their pupils off-piste. Skiing for him was always at best the exploration of untracked mountains, and he derided those who kept to beaten pistes.

He wrote to Friedl Wolfgang, as President of the Downhill-Slalom Committee, and Peter Kasper, President of the Swiss Ski Instructors Association, in an effort to get ski racing and ski teaching adapted to the mountains, rather than adapting the mountains to racers and skiers by grooming them and teaching only on piste. The arguments for the ballpole slalom were still falling on deaf ears.

He was still concerned with safety and wanted 'Technical Delegates' appointed outside the Downhill-Slalom Committee – specifically he wanted Ernst Gertsch to be allowed to act as Technical Delegate for the A-K. He was also rather shocked to find that the course at Sestriere, on which it had been planned to run the Arlberg-Kandahar downhill, had not been homologated by the FIS. The race had been moved to Sestriere because the date had been altered to 1 April and Murren was unlikely to have sufficient snow so late in the season. Jimmy Palmer-Tomkinson's sons were beginning to follow in their father's ski tracks and Lunn was glad to see Charles racing bravely in the A-K. After the A-K, Lunn went to Adelboden and was wondering if he should give up skiing. At the end of April he was staying at Kleine Scheidegg, then from 27-30 in Zurich, followed probably by a visit to the Prince and Princess of Liechtenstein. An A-K Committee Meeting was held in Zurich in June, to put together A-K and FIS rules covering racers who competed hors concours, the appointment of juries, etc.

As well as sorting out the Year Book, deciphering Lunn's typing and generally coping with the chaos of his papers, Phyllis Holt-Needham was contributing small and entertaining articles of her own - book reviews, hints on good woolly washing powder, descriptions of the mountains, etc. As Colonel Bowdler had died in January, her contribution was all the more essential. However, at the end of the Review of the Year Lunn announced her retirement.

For nine years after resigning as his Secretary she had agreed to help with the Year Book. At first she had been very diffident in suggesting amendments, but was persuaded that, as they were both very busy, she should not hesitate to speak her mind. Lunn said: "From defects in my prose, she passed by natural transition to defects in my character." It is true that she could, without offence, sort out some of the problems caused by his absentmindedness. Initially shy by nature, she deftly brought out the best in him while making him aware of the needs of others.

He visited the Swiss Institute for Mountain Research, who had commissioned "A Century of Mountaineering" and, more recently, an essay on Geoffrey Winthrop Young to appear in the next issue of Mountain World. Fraulein Spichiger, Secretary of the Institute, watching him walk blindly into the Zurich traffic while cars screeched to a halt, remarked: "I wonder you have remained unkilled for so long". This so pleased Lunn that he recommended it as the title for anyone who wrote his biography, but he anticipated them by writing his memoirs with that title in 1968.

13

1961-63 Fighting Shamateurism and Marriage to Phyllis

1961 STARTED WELL when Lunn received a letter from the President of the Alpine Club, asking him if he would accept Honorary Membership. He was duly elected on 12 February and, after the struggle he had had to join the Club, the honour was all the more appreciated.

The British Men's Downhill Championship was held in Murren and attracted the usual enthusiastic entry. Philippa Hussey, who was Race Secretary, nearly threw two of the entries into her wastepaper basket as hoaxes when they appeared in the names of the Aga Khan and Winston Churchill. Fortunately, they were rescued in time, for Prince Karim and young Winston (grandson of the Prime Minister) duly arrived and competed.

Lunn was particularly pleased when the Town Teams race for the Infante Alfonso Cup was won by Bern. The team consisted of two Obrechts and two Kaechs – sons of the winners of the first Duke of Kent Cup in 1937.

There was more friction at this time between Lunn and Field Marshal Montgomery. They disagreed over which events British racers should enter. Lunn felt it was best to win in Citadin and Lowlander events than come last in top FIS races. Montgomery encouraged them to go to FIS races, where they could, if successful, gain international points. In February, there was some sharp correspondence between them when Montgomery was quoted in the Observer as saying to Lunn: "Because you invented the slalom in the Stone Age, it does not mean that you have the right to pontificate, legislate and hold things the way they have always been. The Old Guard are against change and progress and are suffering from a high degree of mental constipation." He added that he: "Would like to administer a strong dose of weedkiller to whoever stopped full teams being entered for all the top races."

Lunn wrote, taxing him with the quotation and saying that he should have been raising funds for British racers rather than for Swiss schoolboys. Montgomery had encouraged races between the boys of Murren and those of Wengen. The two men had never got on well. Montgomery did rely a lot on Robert Readhead, who had taken Lunn's place on the FIS Council and who, Lunn felt, acted in his own interests rather than those of British racers. A letter of April 1960 to Rosemary Tennant was critical of Robert Readhead's self-interest: "Did you read Robert's reports? I do like a man who runs true to form."

Major Ted Varley of Murren had given Montgomery good advice, but without result. Varley was the son of a British Army Officer who had been interned in Murren during the First World War. Ted also served in the British Army during the Second World War, married Aliki, from Greece, and they formed an invaluable link between Murren village and the Kandahar.

The Arlberg-Kandahar was held on 10-12 March in Murren, where they were celebrating fifty years as a winter sports centre. Lunn praised the organisation, despite the fact that manpower was a problem. Murren, with a big reputation but small in size, had only 800 beds, compared with 3,000 or 4,000 at most ski resorts. This made finding people for piste preparation and gatekeeping difficult. But Murren's resources, coordinated by Ted Varley, were enough to cope with all the problems.

Bill Bracken had died. After the A-K races, Helen Tomkinson, Walter Amstutz and Jimmy Riddell (now married to Jeannette Kessler) scattered Bracken's ashes over the downhill course. Lunn was made Patron of the

Curling Club of Murren and in an inaugural speech he said: "Knowing nothing about curling, I was diffident about taking this on, but I consoled myself with the reflection that Field Marshal Montgomery accepted the Presidency of the Kandahar Ski Club. One thing you can be sure of, I shall not recommend concentrated doses of weedkiller for the Committee."

Lunn wrote to Rosemary Tennant, asking that Adelboden should be supported by the Ski Club of Great Britain. He reminded her that in 1902 Adelboden had seen the birth of English ski racing. The Public Schools Alpine Sports Club Cup, the predecessor of the Roberts of Kandahar, had been held there and he had himself won the Cup in 1903.

Martini & Rossi were planning to sponsor Kandahar races. The Martini International Club had been formed 'to promote and encourage top-class sporting and cultural events'. In motor sport they sponsored the Aston Martin Owners Club and they considered the Kandahar Ski Club was the skiing equivalent. Lunn's links with Giovanni Nasi were helpful. Philippa Hussey, as Secretary of the Kandahar Ski Club, had met Martini's representatives at the Chamonix A-K. Major John Covernton, Martini's Managing Director in London, explained that they were willing to put £10,000 into the races over a period of five years.

On 18 April, Lunn married Phyllis Holt-Needham – the date chosen was his birthday so that, Phyllis said, he should not forget it. It was a very successful marriage for the two understood and appreciated each other well. It also made all the difference to their friends for Lunn by himself was untidy and disorganised. With Phyllis to look after him, the ingenuity, wit and charisma of the 'helpee' flourished.

She was given useful advice and warnings by many of Lunn's friends. The Infanta Beatrice asked if she had much trouble with Lunn's false tooth. After staying at the Palace during the Civil War he had written to say he had left behind his overcoat, his missal and his tooth, and that if they would forward the missal and tooth the coat could be used in the Infanta's relief work. She had given the coat to a bank manager who had been successfully hidden from the Reds, but had all his clothes stolen.

Lunn continued his battle to make racing a test of mountain skiing and avoid the rhythm that tightly set courses imposed on racers. He advocated what he called 'alpine figures', where a racer had to choose a line between two gates, rather than 'cresta figures', whereby all racers were forced to turn at exactly the same point. He went with James Riddell to Interlaken to a Downhill-Slalom Committee chaired by Friedl Wolfgang, who said they intended to try out alpine figures, but Lunn complained that they never did so.

The FIS dropped the word amateur from their qualification for racers, but still banned those whose victories were used in advertisements by their equipment suppliers. Lunn wrote to Avery Brundage, making it clear that top racers were accepting money to race. This did not happen in the classic downhills such as the A-K, Lauberhorn and Hahnenkamm, but where villages wanted to attract big crowds and knew that Olympic racers would be a draw. Brundage was insisting that three officials had to sign an amateur form before a racer could be entered for the Olympics, and therefore the Federations were at fault rather than the IOC if competitors were not true amateurs. Lunn felt it was absurd to pretend that anyone who trained throughout the year, as top racers had to do in order to win, could be considered an amateur.

Meanwhile a successor to Phyllis Holt-Needham had to be found as Assistant Editor of the British Ski Year Book. Rosemary Tennant wrote from the SCGB to say she was sure that Lunn would like Christobel Haward. She was an author and journalist in her own right, the Latin American advisor to a new magazine called 'El Sol', and was just completing a book on the Andes.

She was appointed, but Lunn did not find her quick to respond to his letters. In June he wrote to complain to Rosemary Tennant, who had herself been very busy organising the building of a ski jump at Wembley Stadium, covering it with crushed ice and arranging an international jumping competition.

For some time a painting of trees in blossom by Adrian Allinson had been lent by Lunn to the SCGB. Living now in Phyllis Lunn's small flat in

Archery Fields, London, he decided to bequeath the painting to the SCGB and they accepted with grateful thanks. Allinson had been a member of the Club from 1929-40 and from 1954-58. Lunn also wrote to the Club recommending that James Riddell should be awarded the Pery Medal, saying that no-one had explored the Alps more thoroughly on ski.

Lunn still acted as the SCGB's representative in Switzerland and, as such, he sent regular reports to Council. In them he tended to ride his hobbyhorses and Council members complained about the length of the reports that he expected them to read and discuss.

Christobel Haward was ill during the final stages of preparing the Year Book for the press, and as a result it came out late. Lunn was not happy, but sympathised and said that lowered vitality must be due to the difficulties of completing the Racing section.

Rosemary Tennant retired from the Ski Club of Great Britain and Lunn paid her a tribute – not forgetting her line about his visits to the clubhouse, 'the Knight cometh when no man can work'. She had been a vital link between him and the Club over the years. Wise, witty and industrious, she had seen the SCGB through many rough waters. Lunn appreciated her for he would always respond to those who stood up to him, provided their criticisms were right – but they had to be right. Malcolm Milne, recently retired from the Colonial Service, took over as Secretary of the SCGB.

In October 1961 Lunn was making his usual lecture tour in the United States, visiting among other colleges Dartmouth, Notre Dame, Indiana, St Joseph's, West Hartford, Connecticut and Boston. Roland Palmedo drove him to Mad River Glen in New England. It was exactly the sort of resort that he liked best, for the mountain was left in its natural state and the pistes were not groomed.

Dartmouth College had put on an exhibition of his books and a page of manuscript from "A Century of Mountaineering", which he admitted was not easy to decipher. He had invented his own system of speedwriting, which gave anyone trying to type from it a great deal of difficulty. On his way back from the States, he went to Lisbon and gave a lecture for the British Council there on skiing.

By December he was again based in Murren, though busy travelling to races as Skiing Correspondent of The Daily Telegraph. His policy with the British Team was still to encourage them to compete in Citadin races, which they could win, rather than top FIS races where they were now outclassed by racers brought up in the mountains.

The 1962 British Racing Week was held in Davos from 8-14 January. There was not much snow at the beginning of the month, but a good fall came during the night before the giant slalom, providing excellent conditions. Competitors were called on to stamp the course, to make it safe and stop it rutting. Mechanical grooming of courses was still in its infancy.

The Aga Khan was racing for Britain and won the Roberts of Kandahar as well as the Lowlander individual championships. Charles Palmer-Tomkinson won the British Downhill Championships.

Honore Bonnet, Manager of the French Team who brought Jean-Claude Killy and Guy Perillat to beat the rest of the World, had made a film of the downhill at the 1962 Murren A-K, which showed the racers memorising the slalom gates at the top of the course before setting off. Lunn did not see the film until the following season and was then shocked. The race he felt had become a test of memory, no longer a test of skiing fast through trees. To him the slalom racer had become simply an acrobat. He argued that if the controls in a downhill race were set without giving the racer the opportunity to see them, the racer would have to go more slowly and therefore more safely. Elsa Roth, Chairman of the Ladies Committee of the FIS, wrote from Bern to commend his article and to credit Marc Hodler with the idea of a qualifying slalom.

In February, the Daily Mail was enquiring about a rift between Lunn and Lord Montgomery. Lunn wrote to the Editor on 15 February, saying he had made no statement about Monty at Chamonix. The Committee of the Kandahar had agreed that a careful statement should be prepared and only if Montgomery's resignation as President of the Club reached the Press should it be issued. So when The Daily Telegraph rang him, he referred them to the Secretary, Philippa Hussey, saying that as Montgomery was the first cousin of his first wife he was particularly anxious not to be involved in any public controversy. Philippa Hussey told them the Field-Marshal's handover had been back in 1958 and their curiosity subsided. That was also the year in which Montgomery had retired as Deputy Supreme Commander, Allied Powers Europe.

The A-K took place in Sestriere from 9-11 March. Arnold and Phyllis Lunn travelled with Philippa Hussey from Murren, being met by a Fiat car sent by Giovanni Nasi. Karl Schranz of Austria won the A-K Combined for the fourth time in succession. Teams came from Holland, Belgium and Denmark as well as Britain, for whom the Aga Khan was racing. (He wrote to Lunn, asking that he should stay with the racers rather than at a more prestigious hotel.) The course, set diagonally across two gulleys, made careful judgement essential.

Naturally there was a good party afterwards. The British Ambassador, Sir Charles and Lady Taylor, Sir Norman and Lady Roberts, and Prince and Princess Sicherbatov, added lustre to the guest list. Malcolm Milne and Peter Forbes, the SCGB Secretary and Skiing Secretary, attended with their wives. The Lunns spent a couple of days after the race with Etta Bonacossa in Milan. In the last week of March, the Lunns went to the Bahnhof Hotel in Grindelwald. They enjoyed a ride on the 'First' lift and Lunn reflected that, while lifts made skiers lazy, they also made it possible to reach splendid ski-touring country if skiers would only make a short effort to climb from the tops of the lifts. He skied down.

From Grindelwald they went on to Kleine Scheidegg, where they met Joannides, winner of Lunn's first modern slalom in 1922. The snow conditions were excellent at the end of March, with cloudless skies giving sharp frosts at night and sun during the day. There was deep powder from the Scheidegg down to about 1,550m. They dined on their last evening with Fritz and Kasper von Almen.

A few days later Lunn was due to fly to Copenhagen, but thick fog forced the plane to land in Dusseldorf. He lectured for the British Council in Copenhagen and went on to Oslo to lecture to the Anglo-Norse Society on "Mountain and Skiing Memories" and to attend the races for the Holmenkollen-Kandahar Challenge Cup, awarded for a giant slalom and slalom. He was the guest of Bruce Carnall, the Naval Attache at the Canadian Embassy.

The FIS Congress was held in Zurich in May and discussions took place about setting up a Citadin Committee. Rules were proposed, but firm decisions were deferred until the following year.

Phyllis Lunn was concerned about rumours that the SCGB wanted to combine the British Ski Year Book and Ski Notes & Queries. She wrote to Malcolm Milne and pointed out that the Year Book went only to those who paid for it and made a profit of over £500 a year. Also, Lunn had been its Editor since 1920, while Ski Notes & Queries had had many Editors. There was a Council Meeting on 14 June and she hoped the subject would be discussed and that Milne would use his influence to get any hasty decisions postponed. They were to be in Rome, where Lunn was lecturing, at the time of the meeting, and then going on to work at the Swiss Foundation for Alpine Research in Zurich, returning to England around 25 June. In the end, no decision was made at the Council Meeting.

When the Year Book appeared, Lunn was inveighing again about what he called 'selective indignation', which allowed 'Reds' to compete although their racers were not amateurs. He made the point that if South African sportsmen were excluded because of Apartheid, then communist competitors should also be excluded. He again deplored the way slaloms were set with Cresta figures, which forced them all to turn on the same spot.

At 74 Lunn still had all his old drive and competitive spirit, but he showed his age by being very repetitive and obsessed with his pet subjects: rules, amateurism and slalom setting. He quoted De Coubertin's description of amateurism as "Wonderful Mummy" many times. He often justified his obsessions, quoting Lord Northcote as saying that you had to repeat a thing ten times before anybody heard what you said, and a hundred times before anybody believed it.

An obituary for C. Scott Lindsay set Lunn reminiscing back to 1907, when he and his brother Hugh spent the summer in Montana and first met Scott Lindsay. They had also visited Norway together before he met

Mabel, and it was thanks to Scott Lindsay that Lunn's leg had not been amputated after his fall.

Scott Lindsay had spent some time in Malta during the war in Army Intelligence. Like Lunn, he appreciated the beauty of the mountains. He had written: "No man who has breathed the chill air of the dawn on the glaciers, that cold blast that always precedes the day, can doubt that there are eternal values which sustain man in his every purpose, whatever his creed or colour."

On 4 December 1962 Lunn was in Spokane, but Phyllis reported that he would soon be going with her to the Palace Hotel in Murren. She expected, rightly, that he would be away a lot reporting on racing for The Daily Telegraph.

There was a British Ski Racing Week in Val d'Isere from 8-13 January 1963. The A-K was in Chamonix from 8-10 March. Marc Hodler attended and Digby Raeburn, now a General, flew in to serve on the Slalom Jury. He was Chairman of the British Ski Racing Committee. As usual, Lunn remembered to thank everyone in his report in the Year Book.

He felt that the points system could be improved for combined events. In 1936 slalom points counted as five-eighths of downhill points, but in 1963 they counted as five-sixths of downhill points. It was important that the start order for the slalom should be determined by the finishing order in the downhill.

It was becoming obvious that racers such as Karl Schranz, who used Kneissl skis, were paid by manufacturers because they gave such good publicity to their products.

Lunn at last achieved his ambition to reach the top of Mont Blanc. During the A-K at Chamonix, Monsieur Couttaz, President of the Development Society, offered to arrange a helicopter flight, which took place in September. Lunn arrived on 17 September in Chamonix and on the 18th Couttaz had the helicopter ready for him. There was not a cloud in the sky at 8.30am when he was driven to the helicopter pad. The Press and television were present. At 10am they reached the summit. Lunn enthused:

"I felt as if I were flying not only through space, but also through time, airborne back to the mountains of my youth. Shortly after taking off, the first slope down which I had slid and tumbled on ski appeared below, the Aiguille du Tour, my first peak, rose above a shoulder of the Brevent, and then in swift succession the mountains of memory occupied the eastern sky, the beloved Oberland, the Combin, the last mountain that I had climbed with two legs of the same length, the Dent Blanche; the first painful return to the High Alps after my smash and then, as the helicopter turned towards the east, the Gouter, the last peak I shall ever climb on my legs. Now at last the haunting sense of failure, which the sight of Mont Blanc has evoked in me since my check on the Gouter, will be mitigated by the modified satisfaction of having at least set foot on the summit."

He also wrote for The Tablet, the Catholic weekly edited by his friend, Tom Burns: "I gave thanks to the great architect for the chief things of the ancient mountains and the precious things of the lasting hills". In February 1963, Lunn had been skiing for three days running with great energy.

Christobel Haward suffered from pleurisy in January. Lunn wanted her to visit the Bernese Oberland, but she said Malcolm Milne was unable to fund her from the SCGB and she could not afford to pay her own way. Lunn suggested that she could travel on the SCGB charter flight and the Swiss Tourist Office might fund her while in Switzerland. He talked to Godi Michel, but she was not anxious to stay away for the two weeks he suggested. He was increasingly impatient about the time she took to reply to his letters and requests.

However, in February she went into hospital with bronchial asthma and was still there in the middle of March. In April she was working mainly from home, and Lunn complained that she scribbled messages to him on the backs of envelopes which he couldn't read. By 4 June Malcolm Milne reported that she was back working four hours a day, five days a week. Lunn sent Milne a stream of complaints, but said not to pass them on for he did not want her upset after being so ill.

The Ski Club of Great Britain was finding it increasingly difficult to fund the ski teams. In 1963 the Club had spent about £6,000 on alpine racing. Only £1,400 came from business and private donations, the rest had to be taken from members' subscriptions. But the Club needed the subscription revenue to provide facilities for members and attract new ones. Racers were no longer rich enough to pay the very considerable travel and accommodation costs, which built up as they drove themselves from race to race. Teams from alpine countries were provided by their Federations with trainers, managers and equipment, as well as comfortable travel and accommodation. Either sponsors must be persuaded to cover costs, or a way must be found to tap into grants available from the Central Council of Physical Recreation and the Ministry of Education. As a members' club, the SCGB could not qualify for grants. The President set up a Steering Committee to study the problem.

Lunn complained later that every SCGB Committee Meeting to discuss the foundation of a new Federation was held during the six months when he was absent from England, first in America and then in the Alps, and that during those six months not one letter was addressed to him by the President of the Ski Club.

Always taking a lively interest in the running of the SCGB, coupled now with the possible setting up of a National Federation, Lunn wrote every few days to Milne, as well as sending his reports as Swiss Representative to Council. He gave his views on the precarious situation of SCGB Reps in resorts, the necessity of keeping the Information Service available only to members, the privileges given to associated clubs, and the importance of the SCGB remaining the governing body of skiing. Any future Federation must be involved only in racing.

He suggested that a new body should be called the National Ski Racing Council. The SCGB must continue to appoint the Chairman of the Council and its Subcommittees, Representatives, Test Judges and the Editor of the magazine.

An Editor was sought to take over from Colonel 'Bunny' de Linde, who had for years edited the Year Book's sister journal Ski Notes & Queries.

Christobel Haward was not well and Lunn vehemently opposed the idea that she should take on the job as she was not a skier. He was still complaining that she did not do what he asked. But she was appointed and Ski Notes & Queries was changed from its original pocketbook format to quarto, making it more attractive to advertisers. Lunn had been writing hard. "The Swiss and their Mountains", commissioned by the Swiss Foundation for Alpine Research, was published in 1963 and also "The Englishman on Ski". In a preview to the latter, printed in the1962 Year Book, Lunn explained that it was to celebrate the Diamond Jubilee of the Ski Club of Great Britain. It outlined the many contributions made by Englishmen to the sport, in all its aspects from ski-mountaineering to ski-racing.

Lunn was talking further to Giovanni Nasi and Major John Covernton of Martini, about setting up the Citadin Committee with a circuit of races to include the Sestriere Derby, the Kandahar-Martini and an Austrian race.

The Lunns were in Murren at the Palace until it closed on 25 March, and then stayed at the Eiger Hotel for a week. Peter and Marguerite Hofmann of the Hotel du Lac in Interlaken, gave a dinner to celebrate his 75th birthday – it also celebrated the 75th anniversary of the Hotel being taken over by the Hofmann Family. Godi Michel and his wife Louise and Kaspar von Almen and his wife Erika were there, as well as the Lunns. Then on 18 April, Fritz von Almen entertained them at the Scheidegg. They spent Easter with Jacqueta Lunn, who was working in Geneva.

Lunn was still deploring false amateurism – it would be better, he thought, to turn professional than to pretend to be an amateur. He praised the Pro League, which had been set up by Stein Eriksen, Tony Spiess, Christian Pravda and Anderl Molterer.

Always interested in changing rules to improve racing, he approved of the idea of the FIS allowing each country a quota of racers. At that time there was no system of awarding points to racers on a yearly basis, so he suggested listing the best racers for A and B circuits – which, at Serge Lang's instigation, were to become the World Cup and Europa Cup circuits.

Lunn explained his priorities when collecting articles for the Year Book. Each must be written by an authority on its subject. It was not important that an article should interest every reader, but the experts in its particular field must enjoy it. So ski-mountaineering, competition, technique, equipment, even book reviews all made interesting reading to somebody. Among the subjects he listed was controversy, and perhaps this was his favourite. It was certainly the subject to which he devoted most space.

From 26-30 April the Lunns were staying with the Prince and Princess of Liechtenstein at Schloss Vaduz. In "The Skier" of 1961 (a British ski magazine to which he contributed a regular column) Lunn quoted the Princess of Liechtenstein who once remarked to him: "When I tell the servants that Sir Arnold is coming, they give a tired smile." Then they went to the Hotel Helvetia at the Venice Lido from 1-6 May, then to the Hotel Madrid in Rome for a couple of weeks before returning to Murren, where they stayed with the Varleys at their Chalet Schneeflockli.

While in Rome, at a party given by the Millington Drakes, they met Elisabeth Hussey, whose sister Philippa had been Secretary of the Kandahar Ski Club for many years. Elisabeth Hussey had recently left Autocar magazine and was spending some months in Rome working for the UN's World Food Program. Phyllis Lunn suggested that she might call in at Murren to see them on her way home in November.

The first FIS Citadin Subcommittee meeting took place in Belgium on 26 October 1963. Roland du Roy de Blicquy of Belgium was made President and brought firsthand knowledge from following his daughter Patricia's progress on the racing circuit. Helen Tomkinson represented Britain, but Lunn sat in as an observer and made some suggestions. He did not want his Kent races to be included, as he was determined not to have to invite communist countries to send teams. In the end, it was agreed that the organisers of Citadin races did not have to follow the normal FIS rule of inviting all nations. He also felt this should be a full Committee, not a Subcommittee of the FIS.

He agreed that the support and recognition of the FIS would be of great value in persuading tourist offices to treat these races seriously. He was, however, totally against the proposed FIS rule to include racers who had previously lived in the mountains but spent the last three years in a town. The whole point of the new circuit was to eliminate those brought up in the mountains. Citadin racing was established as an FIS circuit that winter.

Lunn was still very interested in Moral Rearmament and in August he and Phyllis went to Caux above Montreux, to stay in Moral Rearmament's Mountain House. He enjoyed the discussions, but Phyllis found the atmosphere stifling and longed to return to what she called 'less woolly theology'. Lunn was writing "The New Morality" with Garth Lean. By the following summer it had sold 250,000 copies. It was dedicated to Geoffrey Appleyard, a ski racer who went missing in parachute operations during the war and who was Garth Lean's brother-in-law.

During the annual lecture tour of America in the autumn, Lunn caught up with many friends. He was staying with the Palmedos at the time of the Cuba crisis. In New York, he met Silvia Sella and stayed with Helen McAlpine, who had raced for the USA in the 1936 Innsbruck Massacre. After some weeks in the Mid West, he flew to Denver and met Jerry Hart who, as a Rhodes Scholar, had been Secretary of both the Oxford Mountaineering and Ski Clubs.

In November, at the end of his lecture on skiing and mountaineering, Dudley Smith, who had introduced him, said: "During the war Sir Arnold gave us a talk which was mainly about mountaineering and skiing, but he also showed some slides of the Battle of Britain and seemed to think that it would be a good thing if we Americans came over to Europe where he could offer us a sport more exciting than mountaineering and skiing". From Denver Lunn went on to Los Angeles, staying as guest of Stan Mullin, Vice-President of the FIS.

He also attended the Silver Jubilee celebrations of Timberline Lodge on Mount Hood in Oregon, to which he had contributed a prize in 1938. There he recalled his last visit in 1958, when he had met two girls on a train. "My friend", said one of them, "won a race on Mount Hood, Oregon, called the Arnold Lunn Cup." "Why is it called that?" Lunn asked. "Oh it's called after a prehistoric skiing guy. He's been dead a mighty long time, I guess." Lunn commented that some people might feel slightly relieved if that guess were correct.

He was amused by the following paragraph, which appeared in a local paper:

"Timberline Lodge displayed more dignitaries Sunday than a Kennedy swimming-pool party. Top federal and civic officials spoke their pieces at either the new lift dedication, the Lodge's 25th Anniversary Celebration, or the High-Mountain Conference that followed. But it was a peppery elderly Englishman who stole the show – Sir Arnold Lunn. Sir Arnold has a sharp wit, laced with a love of controversy, a background in skiing second to none, and an appreciation of people. Mount Hood skiers took him right to their hearts."

Lunn was always ready to take the opportunity to sell copies of the British Ski Year Book and so reduce its cost to the Ski Club. Roland Palmedo suggested that they should be marketed through the ski clubs in the States. He helped by providing a list of clubs and the President of the United States Ski Association, Dr Merritt Stiles, ordered a hundred copies for sale at their Annual Meeting in San Francisco. Sadly these were not posted from the SCGB until January so Lunn's opportunity was wasted.

Until this issue, the Year Book had been sent only to those club members who paid extra for it. From 1963 onwards it was posted to every member as part of their club subscription. Under the old system of accounting, it had showed a yearly profit of about £600 for the Club, but in future stopping the extra charge and with the increase in printing and postage costs it appeared in the Club's accounts as a loss. At a Council Meeting on 28 November 1963 a Publications Committee was set up to consider an eventual successor to Sir Arnold. Lunn insisted that any Editor must be a skier, know French and German, and represent Great Britain on the FIS. He said he hoped to edit 50 issues of the Year Book – which would take him to 1969.

Phyllis Lunn, always working in the background to help Lunn, suggested that Elisabeth Hussey should be interviewed by the SCGB with a view to her working as the Assistant Editor of both the Year Book and Ski Notes & Queries.

At the FIS there were also changes. Robert Readhead lost his seat on the Council to Czechoslovakia. Lunn was angry at Britain having no representation and complained that far too many seats were now in the hands of the communists.

14

1964-69 Ski Racing Organization and 80th Birthday

Lunn went to the British Men's Alpine Championships, held with the Lowlanders and the Duke of Kent Cup in Val d'Isere from 3-10 January 1964. Digby Raeburn was there to officiate. In the 1960's few British ever went to Val d'Isere and the Mayor, Monsieur Machet, was farseeing and generous in providing its superb courses and race organisation free of charge for British organisers. The resort reaped the benefit in excellent publicity when the racers explored the extensive and challenging slopes and told their friends at home about them. Soon British holidaymakers were coming in their thousands and voting it their favourite resort.

The 1964 Olympic Games took place in Innsbruck between the end of January and 9 February. Mindful of the accidents at the Innsbruck World Championships of 1936, and John Semmelink's death in Garmisch in 1959, Lunn had complained the year before that the courses were to be held through trees. In mitigation, it had been argued that the light and wind shelter was better in the woods. Sadly, his warning was fulfilled when an Australian, Ross Milne, was killed while practising for the downhill.

Lunn went on to the Arlberg-Kandahar at Garmisch from 14-16 February. The Martini International Club donated £500. He acknowledged their generosity, but would not allow the race to be called after them.

To solve the financial difficulties of supporting the British teams, the National Ski Federation of Great Britain (NSFGB) was set up on 11 March. There was a great deal of ill-feeling at the Inaugural Meeting. As a federation of clubs, each club had equal representation. Lunn felt it should be responsible only for ski racing, but all his efforts came to nothing. It was to cover "national activities which concern beginners to the sport and racers." It was to deal with the Central Council for Physical Recreation, and would qualify for grants for the development of skiing as a sport.

The NSFGB settled into the top floor of 118 Eaton Square, under the same roof as the SCGB. Malcolm Milne moved upstairs to act as its Secretary, while Anthony Trappes-Lomax took his place on the SCGB. Digby Raeburn, who had chaired the SCGB Racing Committee, became Chairman of the new Federation's Alpine Racing Committee. Robin Brock-Hollinshead also moved from Club to Federation to become National Coach.

There was already a Scottish Ski Federation. All 52 active ski clubs in the country joined the new Federation, which took from them an annual revenue of one shilling per member. The total came to £2,000, of which the SCGB's share was £685, a considerable improvement on the £6,000 it had been costing them to fund the teams.

On 8 May Malcolm Milne wrote to Lunn in Rome, to say that Christobel Haward had given up her appointment as Editor of Ski Notes & Queries and Assistant Editor of the Year Book. Richard Hennings, a retired Colonial Administrator and friend of Malcolm Milne, was appointed Editor of Ski Notes & Queries. He was an experienced ski-mountaineer and author, as well as a member of both the Alpine Club and Alpine Ski Club. Elisabeth Hussey was appointed Assistant Editor for both publications and started work on 20 May. Phyllis Lunn reported in June that her husband was well pleased and she wrote offering help, but saying she was anxious not to interfere. She was indeed immensely helpful.

On 14 June the Lunns were in Zermatt, then went on to Murren and finally back to London. In July Lunn lunched with Major Covernton at the Athenaeum, to discuss the Martini sponsorship.

Lunn continued to cover racing in the British Ski Year Book, as the new body did not have a journal of its own. For some issues he included a report from the current President of the NSFGB. Marc Hodler, now on the International Olympic Committee, patiently gave a long interview into a tape recorder. Lunn published it together with his continuing thoughts on ski racing:

1. Alpine figures rather than Cresta: Hodler approved of setting courses that gave racers the chance to vary their line though the gates. But he said that whenever Alpine figures were used, as they often were, racers still tended to turn on exactly the same spot, and exaggerated Alpine figures with long drops between gates could cause courses to rut badly.
2. Ballgate slalom poles: Lunn had tried these out at Murren with varying degrees of success. He still felt they were a better way of judging the skill of skiing through woods than poles, which could be pushed out of the way. But Hodler said the balls tended to loosen as one racer went by, then fall out as a second racer passed whether they hit it or not.
3. Lunn insisted that the FIS Downhill Slalom Committee should be made to try out new ideas. Hodler defended the Committee, saying they were very innovative and in fact were often criticised for changing the rules too often.
4. Lunn still wanted racers to tackle slaloms without studying them first, but Hodler explained that it was almost impossible to prevent racers seeing a course before they started their run, and trainers could now use radios to send messages up about the course.
5. Russia, the Alpine nations and America were all represented on FIS Council, but not the Lowlanders. Hodler agreed that all groups should be represented.

Peter Lunn had been posted to the British Embassy in the Lebanon, enjoying the opportunity to be in a place where it was possible to ski and swim on the same day.

On 2 October, Lunn wrote to Trappes-Lomax at the SCGB from the Mountain House at Caux, asking that the Club should sanction his proposals on alpine racing and forward them to the new Federation. The new Secretary sent a rather nervous note to Milne, his predecessor, asking if they could discuss the matter. After a good deal of debate between the two of them and John Howkins, then Chairman of the SCGB, it was decided that Lunn's paper should be discussed at a Council Meeting on his return and then put to the Federation.

Lunn's paper pointed out that as British racers could no longer compete in world-class races, they should concentrate on Citadin events. He agreed to them competing in the Olympics, where the quota of four racers per country meant the British were in competition with fewer racers from Alpine countries and where parents might be pleased to pay expenses. He was anxious to get a good entry for the Kandahar Citadin Race to impress Martini and seal the sponsorship. The Kandahar-Martini Citadin Races were to become the top event in the Citadin calendar from 1966 to 1992.

Lunn resented the amount of money paid by the SCGB to the Federation. Trappes-Lomax was besieged with long, fairly chaotic papers about ski racing, which Lunn requested should be circulated to Council. He attended the meeting in the autumn, but then produced another paper, again suggesting that racers should only be entered in Olympic and Citadin races.

After a spell in Madrid, the Lunns went to Valladolid, then to Seville and back to the Hotel Velasquez in Madrid. He was pleasantly surprised that the Spaniards had not forgotten him. A private car was put at his disposal and it was carefully explained to him that, as he had been awarded the Grand Cross, his title was Excelentismo. Ruefully he admitted in a letter to Elisabeth Hussey that: "Any tendency towards 'Exmoishness' is rapidly checked by Frau Exmo – who sends her love to you." They flew back to London at the end of October.

The link with Martini & Rossi was important. They were initially interested in sponsoring the Arlberg-Kandahar, but Lunn's interest in the Kent races and their successors, the Citadin races, channelled a useful amount of money that way.

It was in October that the SCGB first debated the idea of a merger between the British Ski Year Book and Ski Notes & Queries. Lunn wrote saying: "It is very distressing for me to give up the BSYB in its present form, but if inevitable I must acquiesce."

Foyles held an Exhibition of Kleinmeisters at their Charing Cross Road shop on 11 November. Lunn had been collecting these small coloured engravings of Swiss views in the late eighteenth and early nineteenth centuries for some time, and many of those exhibited belonged to him. He opened the Exhibition with a talk on the genre, and included a chapter on them in "The Swiss and their Mountains".

Lunn was still skiing occasionally – or ski-walking as he called it. In Murren he kept his skis stacked ready for use in the corner of his bathroom at the Palace Hotel. But he complained of increasing difficulty in remembering names and said it was a real help if people said who they were. He blamed old age and panic, but in fact he had always had this problem and Phyllis Lunn assured him that it was really due to overwork and unnecessary controversy.

He wrote, the other day she brought me an advertisement for that admirable institution The Distressed Gentlefolk's Association, with a picture of an old lady murmuring 'At 76 I cannot fight life's battles'. "Many people", said my wife, "would be very relieved if at 77 you stopped fighting your particular battles."

Phyllis Lunn softened the excellent advice she gave him with humour and affection, but they had some great battles. She would try to intercept the articles he sent to the printers, so that names and dates could be corrected, but he often foiled her attempts. He acknowledged that she was right, but still got carried away with his enthusiasm for controversy. She complained that his typewriter was worse than a mistress in distracting him and taking his time. She herself was quiet in company. "I like to listen to the best noise available, and I generally feel I am unlikely to be it", she would say.

Herbert Schneider, who had taken over as Director of his father's ski school in North Conway, attended the 1965 Arlberg-Kandahar, which was held in St Anton from 15-17 January. At the end of the Ladies Downhill, which was won by Annie Famose of France, photographers crowded around Lunn and clamoured for a photograph. Lunn said afterwards that he hoped it would be the last time in his life that he had to be instructed to kiss an attractive girl with thirty cameras pointing at him. The Princess of Liechtenstein was there to present the prizes.

There were celebrations in Murren on 12 March at the opening of the Schilthorn cablecar from Stechelberg to Birg. Lunn enjoyed the view, which had been familiar to him long before when Birg could only be reached on foot. It brought back many happy memories.

He was continuing his interest in Moral Rearmament and writing "The Cult of Softness", which appeared in 1966.

Zermatt was celebrating the centenary of the first ascent of the Matterhorn and Lunn was, of course, invited there. He had written "Matterhorn Centenary" and thanked Karl Weber and the Swiss Institute for Alpine Research for their generosity, which had ensured that the book was beautifully illustrated. He admitted that, though he had the greatest respect for Whymper both as a mountaineer and as author of the alpine classic "Scrambles in the Alps", he did not admire him as a man.

All Lunn's negotiations with the Martini International Club bore fruit when the first Kandahar-Martini Citadin Races took place in Murren in January 1966. Thanks to the expertise of the Kandahar team headed by Helen Tomkinson, with Guy Chilver Stainer of Scotland running the race office, the event became the most popular Citadin race on the circuit. The historic setting of Murren was followed by other venues used for the Arlberg-Kandahar, so that the race also circulated between St Anton, Garmisch Partenkirchen, Chamonix and Sestriere.

Later, at Martini's request, the events were held in northern Italy, near the company's Turin headquarters, so they were based in Courmayeur,

Sestriere and Cervinia. Martini was generous with funds and help with Press coverage, and the sponsorship only ended after 25 years when the FIS banned sponsorship by companies connected with alcohol or cigarettes.

The Kandahar-Martini Citadin Races brought together the Duke and Duchess of Kent Giant Slaloms and the Alpine Ski and Lady Mabel Lunn Slaloms. The Infante Alfonso Cup and the Elsa Roth Cup were given for town team races. Lunn insisted that the Kandahar could invite who they wanted, and he was adamant that invitations should not be sent to countries "where sport is subordinate to politics and ideology."

The A-K was held in Murren on 11-13 March and, despite excellent work on the courses, heavy snowfalsl throughout the two days meant that no downhill could be run. Two slaloms were held instead and Jean-Claude Killy won both.

Until this time, working out the combined winner of a downhill and slalom race took time and the expertise of mathematicians. But now three graduates of St Andrews University (Michael Parlett of Shell, Peter McLaren of the University, and Hugh Hunter Gordon of Ferranti Ltd.) used computers to make the calculations simple. The Kandahar adopted their system and demonstrated at its races how accurate and easy to use it was. Eventually the FIS took over the system, refining it gradually over the years.

Murren ran an Alpine Balloon Week during which pilots managed to cross the Alps. Lunn had moved from the Palace Hotel to the Jungfrau Lodge. Before returning to England he spent a night at Wengernalp, where Kaspar and Erika von Almen gave the usual birthday party for him with Godi Michel and "Johan" Joannides. Kaspar von Almen was now the Gemeinde President of Lauterbrunnen. His father Fritz had died that year.

The Times published a letter from Lunn on Shamateurism. John Betjeman saw it and wrote to Lunn on 10 June, saying he had just finished reading "The Harrovians". "It must be the pioneer of realistic school stories and it is packed with memorable scenes."

In 1966 the FIS gave Lunn a Diploma of Merit for services rendered to the development of skiing and assistance given to its activity. But Lunn wrote to Brigadier Gueterbock saying that he wanted no fuss made over the Diploma and he would collect it when convenient, rather than have a special celebratory presentation. He rather hoped that Marc Hodler might present it when he came to London for an SCGB Dinner.

He was still battling with the NSFGB on behalf of the SCGB. On 6 July he wrote: "Most members consider that the Ski Club entrusted the NSF with complete control over British competitive skiing, but remained the governing body for all other aspects of British skiing…..you relegate the SCGB to a position indistinguishable from that of any of the other clubs represented on the NSF." General Sir Roderick McLeod replied: "The Federation has been recognised by Government and is in close touch with the Sports Council, the Education Department and the Central Council of Physical Recreation".

Despite his age – he was now 78 – Lunn gave 14 lectures in the United States during October and November. He crossed the continent from coast to coast, speaking to Catholic groups as well as skiing and mountaineering clubs. It was his 18th lecture tour in the States and Phyllis Lunn's first visit there.

Old friends welcomed them both. They spent a happy weekend at the beginning of the tour with William and Patricia Buckley. Bill Buckley was the son of a millionaire who defended an uncompromisingly conservative philosophy and spent over two million dollars financing "The National Review", which he had founded ten years before. Buckley had stood for election as Mayor of New York, knowing that there was no chance of being elected. "If elected, I'd demand a recount", he said. It was an attitude that Lunn appreciated.

Roland Palmedo was equally hospitable and they spent an evening with the Kiaers. It was the last time they were to see Alice Kiaer, who died in 1968. Lunn was interested in religious controversy while on his tour and wrote to Elisabeth Hussey: "There is much talk among the traditionalists of 'the Church indignant' and 'the Church embittered'. I always like being in a minority. That was one of the attractions of becoming a Catholic, and now I'm in a minority of that minority but I hope to avoid being excommunicated for orthodoxy."

The second Kandahar-Martini took place in Sestriere from 20-22 January 1967 and to Lunn's satisfaction was a great success for the British. The first five girls in the giant slalom were all British. But he was already predicting that, with the FIS races being divided into A and B categories, it would only be a matter of time before Citadin qualifications were disregarded and this became the third-class C circuit. He also said an Olympic amateur might be defined as a man who is brave enough to lie for his country.

The A-K, celebrating its 40th year, was held in Sestriere from 3-5 March. The Lunns were flown in by helicopter to look at the ladies course, which the Italian army had been enlisted to prepare. Lunn was brought to the finish in a chair and protested that he only accepted because it would have been rude to refuse.

Foreign travel was still restricted, with a £50 limit on taking money out of the country for holidays. But the Alps were preparing for future tourists. On 14 June, the final stage of the cablecar up to the Schilthorn from Murren was opened.

The World Cup, the brainchild of journalist Serge Lang, was founded that year. At nominated events through the season, racers collected points, so that an overall World Cup winner could be announced each year. These events became the most important in each country. This did not help the Arlberg-Kandahar which, because it moved from one country to another each year, became difficult to fit into the FIS calendar.

By October 1967 Colonel Coke had taken over as Secretary of the SCGB. He dealt politely and efficiently with Lunn's frequent attacks on the National Ski Federation.

Lunn made what was to be his last trip to the United States, though he continued to lecture in Britain. In the autumn, he lectured to the Oxford Mountaineering Club and returned to the flat in Archery Fields where he and Phyllis Lunn lived on 26 November. In December he was diagnosed as having cancer of the prostate.

Dr Harold Davis, his doctor and also at that time Chairman of the SCGB, discussed with Phyllis Lunn how the news should be broken to him. But Davis reported afterwards that, far from being intimidated by the thought of cancer, Lunn had been much more interested in talking about the Federation. Phyllis Lunn, usually allergic to skiing politics, said this was the first time she was really grateful to the Federation. Lunn underwent the first of what were to be several operations.

He was not well enough to attend the Kandahar-Martini Citadin races in Garmisch-Partenkirchen at the end of January 1968. He handed over the Chairmanship of the Arlberg-Kandahar committee to Rudi Matt, Head of the St Anton Ski School and an early racer in the A-K. At this stage the A-K centres were not too happy about the idea of a link with Martini - though by 1970 they were more receptive.

On 16 February Lunn was expected in Murren and finally arrived, cheerful but on a stretcher, to be taken to the Jungfrau Lodge. Four days later, however, he was taken to Interlaken Hospital, gravely ill, so missed a planned visit to Chamonix, where the A-K was being held. The resort was celebrating its own 70th Anniversary and wanted to honour Lunn for starting his skiing there and for his 80th birthday. All the A-K clubs were to make presentations to him, but he was not well enough to travel there.

The pound was devalued, making ski holidays expensive. On his birthday in April, Lunn published another book "Unkilled for So Long". It was semi-autobiographical and Tom Burns, an old Catholic friend who was Managing Director of the publishers Burns Oates & Washbourne, said that Lunn: "Was a tempestuous, but ever-welcome intruder at the office. He dished up books of theology and apologetics like fast food, often with the same ingredients. An autobiography would appear in various guises about every two years, but his "Now I See" (1933) deserves a special place among conversion stories. He was an Editor's despair: quotations unchecked, endless repetitions and misspellings in the untidiest of typescripts ever submitted. The package was shoddy, but there was nothing shoddy about Arnold's mind. He was as agile in the upper regions of religious controversy as he was on the ski-slopes of Switzerland, which he had made his own. He would scorn the 'blue-domers' as he called those who drew spiritual inspiration without dogmatic content from the deep blue skies over the mountains, but there can be no doubt that the mysteries of God's creation were also taught wordlessly to him in the alpine peaks" (The Use of Memory, Sheed & Ward).

1968 marked the 60th Anniversary of the Alpine Ski Club. The Club had grown and prospered. Lunn had edited the Alpine Ski Club Year Book for 60 years, incorporating it into the British Ski Year Book in 1920.

Lunn was still at loggerheads with Avery Brundage of the International Olympic Committee over allowing communists to race as amateurs. Avery Brundage insisted that it was up to the FIS to refuse entry to those who were not amateur, but Lunn reposted that the Olympics should be open, to avoid shamateurism. Both agreed that alpine skiing had become a business and it was impossible to stop racers benefitting from the manufacturers who supplied their skis, boots, bindings and clothes.

Typically helpful, Phyllis Lunn wrote on 10 April to Colonel Coke at the SCGB, sending useful data, dates, etc. for him to quote to the Press who might be reporting on Lunn's 80th birthday. She said they would arrive back on 23 April and Arnold would go straight into hospital to be prepared for the next operation at the beginning of May.

On 18 April Godi Michel organised a wonderful birthday party for him at the Jungfrau Hotel in Murren. Among many friends present were Walter Amstutz, Ernst Gertsch, Peter Hofmann, Jimmy and Jeannette Riddell and Harold Davis. Lunn thanked in particular Karl Weber and Rudi Meyer for their hospitality.

A few days later, Lord Silsoe organised a dinner at the Oxford and Cambridge Club in London, at which Lord Wakefield of Kendal spoke. It, too, was a great assembly of friends, including Evelyn Waugh. Lunn was insistent that this should be regarded as a Kandahar Dinner – he was looking forward to an SCGB one to celebrate his long editorship of the Year Book.

He returned to hospital for the fourth operation in four months. On 16 May, Lady Lunn wrote to Colonel Coke, saying Lunn was much better and Dr Davis hoped he would be able to leave the hospital in about a fortnight. In fact, a week later he went home and wrote to the SCGB saying that he was making steady, if rather slow progress. Thanks to increased membership and sales, the circulation of the Year Book had risen to 12,500 copies.

He was made an Honorary Member of the National Ski Hall of Fame in America, the first foreigner to receive this honour.

Writing about Conan Doyle, he said he was an ardent spiritualist who took him to some seances with one of the most famous mediums of the day. Though he did not adopt Conan Doyle's explanation of the phenomena he witnessed, he had always been deeply interested in the paranormal.

In January 1969, London Weekend Television interviewed Lunn while they were covering the Lauberhorn race. The fourth Kandahar-Martini Citadin Races were attended by the Duke and Duchess of Kent in Murren on 18-19 January. The Duke, a keen skier who had competed in Army Ski Association races, was Patron of the Kandahar, and the cup for the giant slalom had been named after his father. It was a happy and relaxed occasion.

The Arlberg-Kandahar was held in St Anton from 31 January to 2 February. Lunn was there and Herbert and Herta Schneider came to lay wreaths with him on Hannes Schneider's memorial.

Meanwhile, in Murren the James Bond movie "On Her Majesty's Secret Service" was being filmed. The Schilthorn cablecar had opened up long and challenging trails to Murren, as well as a wide bowl of intermediate slopes with a T-bar leading up to Birg, the intermediate station. The cameramen were amazed at the stunning backdrop of the mountains. Many Murreners took part in the film as extras or stand-ins where skiing was required. Lunn was interviewed for a special television programme.

All this time Lunn was talking to Marc Hodler and reporting on his discussions in the Year Book. He was sure that the only reason Russians wanted the amateur rules to continue was that they had no intention of keeping them. Avery Brundage too came in for criticism, because he wanted to abolish the Winter Olympics. Hodler agreed: "He never much liked ice and snow and the older he grows the less he likes snow and ice."

Lunn's interest in Moral Rearmament was continuing and, with Garth Lean of the movement, he had written "Christian Counterattack", which appeared in 1969.

In Murren he was able to keep in touch with the modern mountaineers. Ernst Feuz, then General Secretary of the Swiss Foundation for Alpine

Research, had a chalet in Murren and invited him to meet Toni Hiebeler, who had made the first winter ascent of the Eiger north face and the first ascent of the north face of the Ebnefluh. Ernst Feuz himself had a distinguished race record, having been World Champion in the combined langlauf, ski jumping and downhill event in 1930.

Feuz also invited Lunn to meet six Japanese climbers who had achieved the first summer dirittissima ascent of the Eiger. Lunn was surprised to hear that modern extreme climbers wore steel helmets to protect themselves against falling stones. Tenzing of Everest spent a few days in Murren that August. As Head of the Himalayan Mountain Institute, he was organising a course for Sherpas.

Controversy was growing with the National Ski Federation. Were they the governing body of all skiing or just of ski-racing? The Army Ski Association said they should control all British skiing. Lunn, with his usual fairness, published their letter in the Year Book. But there was a great deal of animosity when the Federation set up a test scheme, sponsored by Coca-Cola, which threatened the long-established SCGB tests. Lunn fulminated. Lewis Drysdale, then President of the Scottish National Ski Federation, wrote to say that: "When the Federation was being considered, the Scottish ski clubs collectively made it clear that they had no interest whatever in a 'sham' federation with responsibility for nothing but racing. They insisted that it must be the national ruling body for skiing with full representation to the International Ski Federation, UIPM and Government".

General Ian Graeme, the General Secretary of the NSFGB, even tried to set up a scheme for ski holidays. These were rightly resented as the SCGB worked hard for holiday skiers. There was still a £50 limit on foreign currency for holidays.

There was also controversy over the British Alpine Ski Championships, because the top British racers were away at International Ski Federation races when they were held. The racers said they had to build up their points in order to qualify for FIS races. Lunn, who had organised the first British Alpine Championships in 1921, was not pleased. He wrote: "Our standing in racing will depend more and more on our prestige as organisers. Our racers will, I fear, be increasingly outclassed."

There was more talk of amalgamating the SCGB's two publications. The Year Book's annual circulation was now 12,500 copies and its cost to the club, included postage to members, came to £3,700. Another suggestion, made by the Army Ski Association, was that they might take copies of Ski Notes & Queries, replace the centre pages (devoted to club notices) with their own, and circulate it to their 10,000 members at cost price. But nothing came of this.

Phyllis Lunn made some useful suggestions. She felt it important to keep the words British and Ski in the title of any new publication, tentatively suggesting British Ski Survey. It must keep the international as well as British interest, however, and should contain the Review of the Year as well as articles, correspondence, a novice section with hints about snowcraft, book reviews and an important equipment section.

At the end of April, Arnold and Phyllis drove to the Hotel Seeburg on Lake Lucerne for two weeks' holiday. The hotel was owned by Neil Hogg (brother of Lord Hailsham), who was a keen ski tourer and spent every winter in Grindelwald.

Lunn was re-elected President of the Kandahar and wrote to Walter Amstutz to say he was flattered, as they could have found a younger man. "Fortunately," he said, "the real work is done by the Chairman, Bill Worthy, my job is purely decorative." "You have been undecorative for so long", Amstutz replied with friendly candour, "that to be decorative will be a pleasant change."

The 1969 edition of The British Ski Year Book was the 50th that Lunn had edited and was enthusiastically received. Roland Palmedo wrote from his home in New York: "There is no publication I look forward to receiving with greater anticipation than the British Ski Year Book. But had I known how extra-interesting your 50th was to be, I should have been holding my breath til it came. Most year books and annuals, as well as ski magazines, include articles of a personal nature – travel trips and expeditions – as yours does, but what principally distinguishes yours is the amount of opinion and criticism in it. The BSYB is still outstanding. Congratulations."

Palmedo also offered to write an article about ski stamps for the next issue. Max Aitken wrote from The Daily Express: "The review is better than ever. You are a marvel."

But the Year Book had become very repetitive. Lunn was still battling for Alpine rather than Cresta slalom courses, and for Ballpole slalom gates. And he continued to insist that entry to Kandahar races should be by invitation only, and that invitations should not be sent to countries where sport was subordinate to politics and ideology.

There were preparations for a celebration of sixty years of the Roberts of Kandahar. "The Kandahar Story" was published, giving the history of the club. Lady Lunn kept a watchful eye on the proofs so that the dates, which in "The Story of Skiing" had often been incorrect, were carefully checked.

J.R. Ackerley, Lunn's companion during the war years in Murren, had written a book titled "My Father and Myself" in which he made references to Lunn. An American reader wrote that it reminded her of: "A mocking and amusing fellow with whom I became very thick. He was the second forceful intellectual under whose dominance I fell. His name was Arnold Lunn and with his energetic, derisive, iconoclastic mind and rasping demonic laugh, he was both the vitality and the terror of the community. Lunn lent or recommended me books to read and thus and with his malicious debunking thought opened my mind."

Lunn underwent more operations, but still posed on skis in Murren with four-year-old Ursula Ruegg on the slope where he had set the first modern slalom. George Konig, the photographer, arranged for the picture to appear in the Press.

15

1970-74 "WHEN YOU ARE OVER 80 YOU SHOULD ONLY SKI FOR PLEASURE"

ON 9 JANUARY 1970 Lunn was busy writing to Rob Tillard, by then Secretary of the SCGB, complaining about the post and suggesting ways of publicising the Ski Club centres so that they would be encouraged to host SCGB representatives. He also suggested commemorating in 1971 the 50th Anniversary of the first national championships to include alpine races.

Murren celebrated its 60th winter season from 12-20 January. Godi Michel masterminded the celebrations and the Kandahar Ski Club held a K-week at the same time, to encourage its members to take part. In the Opening Address, Kaspar von Almen, the Lauterbrunnen Gemeinde President, said: "The people, the Berglers, in all five villages are fond of Arnold and would like me to tell him so officially tonight. After watching the professor with suspicion for about half a century, we finally consider him as one of ourselves because of his affection for our mountains."

Lunn told them about taking a bottle of Mauler champagne to the 'Maulerhubel' on full-Moon nights. The combination of the champagne, the full Moon and powder snow used to result in some memorable skiing.

Another cause for celebration during the week was the marriage of Marc Hodler's son Beat to Ted Varley's daughter Chloe. Murren's future was ensured with the interest and affection of a new generation. A magical reception was held in the Schilthornbahn's top station. Guests went up in the cablecar shrouded in mist, only to find sunshine at the top.

Many old friends gathered in Murren during that week, including Walter and Eveline Amstutz, Peter Hofmann, son of Lunn's old friend Walter Hofmann from the Hotel du Lac in Interlaken, Mouse Cleaver, winner of the first Hahnenkamm, Max Amstutz, and Herr Schlunegger from the Palace. The Inferno, also held that week, was appropriately won by Ted Varley's son Royston, and Lunn noticed with pleasure that John Curle (then Ambassador in Liberia) competed, as well as his daughter.

There were many distinguished entries too in a light-hearted over-60s race held during the week. Jimmy Riddell, Rosli Streif, Helen McAlpin and Beryl Spence came first, second, third and fourth. Lunn said he had thought of entering himself, but had been advised by his son Peter: "When you are over 80 you should only ski for pleasure". In fact by this time, though he would occasionally put his skis on, it was more to please photographers wanting to picture him against the background of the first slalom slope, than to ski.

The A-K was held in Garmisch-Partenkirchen from 30 January to 1 February. Karl Rall of the A-K Committee collected the Lunns from Munich and drove them to the Alpenhof Hotel in Garmisch. The slalom had to be cancelled because of bad weather, but Karl Schranz was awarded a Kandahar Diamond K for the second time when he won the downhill. Major Covernton was there to represent the Martini International Club, who contributed many thousands of pounds to the race and sponsored a successful Cocktail Party and Dinner.

On 26 February, there was a small dinner party at the Jungfrau Hotel in Murren to celebrate the fortieth anniversary of the formal recognition by the FIS of the Alpine Rules for Downhill and Slalom. Walter Amstutz, Great Britain's first ally and representative of the Swiss Ski Association at the 1930 FIS Congress, Ernst Feuz, Harold Davis, representing the SCGB,

Rudi Meyer, President of Murren Ski Club, the SCGB's ally in the early days, and Godi Michel, former President of the Swiss Ski Association, were all there. Marc Hodler had intended to come, but snowstorms delayed him. He arrived the next day, with his wife Anna Rosa, to present Lunn with a beautiful Finnish glass bowl.

In March, James Riddell, then President of the SCGB and author of a wide variety of books, chaired a Publications Committee set up by the Club to consider the future of the Year Book and Ski Notes & Queries. Lunn was away, but the other Editors were joined by Chris Ralling, a television-producer friend of Riddell, Kenneth King, the wise long-time Honorary Treasurer of the Club, and Roy Max, then Secretary. Lunn was anxious that the Club should gain prestige from its new publication, as the Year Book had been so important over the years. Richard Hennings was more intent on producing a magazine that the members of the Club should find entertaining and informative. The name "Ski Survey" was chosen, and all agreed that it must become a major benefit to SCGB members.

Max Amstutz invited the Lunns to Engelberg, on their way from Murren to Neil Hogg's Seeburg Hotel. They had a great weekend, with Kurdirektor Charles Christen arranging for them to go up the Titlis railway, from which Lunn could see the Dom above Zermatt and recall his climb in 1917.

There was a lot of snow late that season in the Alps. Murren still had two metres when they left on 9 April and, when Neil Hogg drove them up the road on the Rigi slopes to Seeboden Alp, skiers were still finding snow at 1,030m. Murren was to have snow on the village streets as late as June.

In July, Phyllis Lunn confiscated Lunn's typewriter, insisting that he should take a month's holiday. Starting in Murren, they revisited Grindelwald and Kandersteg, then, with Lady Lunn's sister Mrs Hamilton Smythe, they spent a week in Montana. Back in Britain, James Hutchings was the Guest of Honour at a small party at which were present: Lunn, Editor of the BSYB, Richard Hennings, Editor of Ski Notes & Queries, Elisabeth Hussey, Assistant Editor of both, and Lady Lunn. That year the cost of the publications to the SCGB, including postage to members, came to £4,417.

Lunn made a rare visit to the cinema to watch "The Downhill Racer", a film that appeared that year and which he considered portrayed an authentic background to the life of a racer. Shots of races had been taken on location during the season and he enjoyed recognising the various courses. In a letter published in The Times in December, he repeated his abhorrence of shamateurism.

The Publications Committee met again and Richard Hennings prepared a dummy of "Ski Survey", in which advertisements could be sold. He sent a copy to Lunn for approval.

In January 1971, Lunn was writing to Roy Max asking for his views on the Arlberg-Kandahar to be circulated. In April, he also wrote to point out how important the Year Book had been in the past, quoting a group of Spanish skiers who had told him in 1945 that they enjoyed it. He suggested that the new publication should have only two issues a year, each at least 96 or preferably 112 pages long. The Review of the Year should continue indefinitely, and the Editors must read foreign papers such as the Swiss "Sport", and keep in touch with news abroad, while not forgetting to describe new developments at home, such as artificial slopes.

The Editors met in May. Richard Hennings had got estimates from printers, searched for distributors and sorted out possible contents. There were Olympics to cover in 1972. A major traverse of the Alps from Kaprun to Mont Blanc had been achieved by a British team and it was decided to open Ski Survey with the first part of that story. Chris Ralling had followed the tour with a BBC film crew.

In London in May, Lunn wrote another long paper on the Future of British Ski Racing for Roy Max to circulate to a list of British ski officials, including the Council of the NSFGB, the Kandahar, the President and Chairman of the SCGB, General Sir Roderick McLeod, Colonel Readhead, General Leathes, Lord Hunt, Helen Tomkinson and many others. In it, he deplored the decline of British ski racing and suggested that, as there was not sufficient money to train racers, they should train with other national teams. He insisted that Citadin races should be supported, as they were more likely to exclude communist racers, who were as good as professionals.

In June, when Richard Hennings and Elisabeth Hussey went to the Lunns' flat in Archery Fields House, they were met by an adamant Lunn. Unless the new publication was to be a dignified production of at least 40 editorial pages, he did not want to be associated with it. Hennings reassured him.

The Publications Committee, now chaired by Ted Reid, who was a long-standing member of the Club, sat in June to consider various options. Lunn suggested that the National Ski Federation should pay a contribution in return for race reports and the inclusion of the report of the Federation's Annual General Meeting. By this time he was thoroughly at odds with the Federation and suggested that it should move to Scotland, the only place ski-racing was possible in Britain. Long after his death, the move to Scotland did in fact come about.

In July, Lady Lunn was writing to Elisabeth Hussey to say she thought Lunn had sent his Review of the Year direct to the printers and suggesting that an arrangement should be made with Mr Hutchings to return the copy for checking before it was set in type – to avoid too many corrections at the galley stage! Lunn was still bypassing both her and the SCGB, with expensive results.

In the last Year Book he included a useful list of the achievements of British skiers in international skiing, including first ascents, race organisation and literature. But he also took the opportunity to put again all his views on shamateurism, his row with Brundage, and a good deal of autobiographical matter.

Consoling letters rolled in from Walter Amstutz, General Leathes of the NSFGB, Charles Taylor, President of the British Olympic Association, Sir Kenneth Swan (a survivor of the first British Championships and President of the SCGB from 1911-1913), as well as friends such as James Riddell.

Always supportive of women in skiing (and he agreed to a change from the name Ladies to Womens Championships in this year), Lunn attended a Luncheon for the Ladies Ski Club hosted by Lord Wakefield of Kendal in the House of Lords. The Hon. Mrs Raynsford, daughter of Wakefield, was President of the Ladies Ski Club that year. Maria

Goldberger, Manager of the Womens Team attended. Helen Tomkinson initiated the Lady Blane Award in memory of her mother, who had presided over the LSC from 1960-61. The first award was made to Divina Galica, who in 1968 had narrowly missed a medal in the Grenoble Olympics. Lunn was invited to the Luncheon as Sinister Father of the Club.

Snow conditions, first ascents, broken-time payments given to racers, and the contrast in ski technique between counter-rotation and wedeln were all covered in the last edition of the British Ski Year Book. Lunn was continuing to write for other publications. For the November issue of The National Review, edited by his friend Bill Buckley, he contributed an article on "Humbug for Beginners", largely deriding the false amateurism of communists.

The 1972 Anglo-Swiss Races were followed by an excellent party, with Marc Hodler's speech on ski politics earning praise. But Walter Amstutz told Lunn that his own speech was one of the finest he had ever given, and also moving because it came from the bottom of his heart. Lunn was now writing to Lord Exeter of the British Olympic Association, urging him to fight for amateurism. Chris Chataway, the runner who was also a keen skier, wrote to Lunn, saying he too was in contact with Exeter and asked to quote Lunn. With amendments, Lunn agreed that athletes from capitalist society, with rare exceptions, received money under the counter from the promoters, and those who lived under communist rule had their material needs taken care of by the State. Lunn and Hennings exchanged letters every couple of days, discussing the length of articles, format of race results, even the colour of the cover, which Lunn said must not be red and black as these were Nazi colours.

On 31 March, Lunn was at the Jungfrau Lodge in Murren, from where he went to Kleine Scheidegg on 14 April to celebrate his 84th birthday and wedding anniversary, and then home on 2 May. On 3 May the Ladies Ski Club held their Annual Dinner at the Tower of London. Lunn was invited as Founding Father. Digby Raeburn was now Governor of the Tower, so the evening included the Ceremony of the Keys. Sadly, Jeannette Riddell, a great racer of pre-war days as Jeannette Kessler, had died. Lunn attended her Memorial Service on 16 May.

The British Ski Year Book and Ski Notes & Queries were finally merged into "Ski Survey". In September, Richard Hennings, as Editor, launched the magazine for sale through bookstalls, adding to its distribution to Ski Club of Great Britain members. Hennings had negotiated successfully with designers, distributors and advertising agents, so that it had the highest circulation of any ski magazine in Britain and attracted useful advertisement revenue.

Lunn reluctantly accepted the financial restraints that had made it necessary to discontinue his Editorship of the British Ski Year Book after a record 51 years. He was given the title of Editor-in-Chief of the new publication, and remained determined that there should be as many pages in it as there had been in the Year Book. He felt strongly that British Championships and British-organised races must be covered. Peter Lunn took over the Equipment section. In fact, Ski Survey came out three times a year (September, October and December) to start with, and ran to 64 pages an issue, so there was plenty of space. Within a few years it was so successful that it was also appearing in November and February.

As its Editor, Richard Hennings gave Lunn room to express his views on amateurism. There was a two-page letter to Lord Exeter in the first issue. There were also several pages of 'Review of the Year'. As usual, Lunn vigorously attacked the National Ski Federation for shameful mishandling of the teams.

He was determined to keep some control over Ski Survey and insisted that his Greek quotations should be accurately printed. Lady Lunn had taken over much of his typing by this time, so it was not difficult to transcribe. She also kept track of the engagements he must attend, though she complained that he often forgot to tell her about appointments he had made himself.

In September, he was back in Switzerland, staying at the Hotel du Lac in Interlaken. In October, Heinz von Bidder hosted a Dinner for him in Grindelwald. Chris Ralling's excellent film of the British Traverse of the Alps was televised in December.

In January 1973, a television team came to interview Lunn and spent all day at the Jungfrau Lodge and on the slope behind the Jungfrau Hotel where Lunn had set the 1922 slalom.

Karl Weber and Lunn exchanged reminiscences in February 1973. Weber recalled that they first met early in the 1940's with David Zogg and Fritz Steuri in Grindelwald. He arranged for a car to take the Lunns to St Anton for the Arlberg-Kandahar. Lunn wrote to Rudi Matt in February, congratulating him on the organisation of the A-K. He hoped Matt would ensure that the Golden Jubilee of the race in 1978 would be held in St Anton, saying: "I shall only be 89 and, as yet, I do not feel my age above my neck". But Lunn did suffer a nasty fall when knocked over by a child on a toboggan in Murren that spring.

Lady Lunn wrote to thank Karl Weber for his help and received back from him an assurance: "My friendship with Arnold was always and will always be a very great joy. A very special pleasure is for me the knowledge that you and Arnold feel so well and comfortable in Murren. Let us hope that this will last for many many years to come". But by May Karl Weber was saying he was not well, and on 26 September he died.

An outstanding mountaineer and an Honorary Member of the Alpine Club, Weber had founded the Swiss Foundation for Alpine Research and commissioned "A Century of Mountaineering", which he presented to every member of the Alpine Club. He had subsidised the illustrations for the "Matterhorn Centenary" and "The Swiss & Their Mountains", and partly financed production of the "Kandahar Story". It was he who had arranged for Lunn to live at the Jungfrau Lodge when the rooms in the Palace Hotel where Lunn had lived for so long were demolished. Weber's death was a great blow to Lunn.

Lunn's letter writing continued, however. In April he wrote to Wavell Wakefield, urging him to ensure that Helen Tomkinson was awarded an OBE. In May he was insisting to Harold Davis, Chairman of the SCGB, that the Club was still the governing body of the sport. Prince Chichibu had died and Princess Chichibu wrote to thank Lunn for his kind words about her husband. There was also friendly correspondence with Max Aitken, then Chairman of The Daily Express.

But Lady Lunn was worried about the effects of the bad fall he had had and the death of Karl Weber. She wrote to Philippa and Elisabeth Hussey on 13 October: "I think you will find Arnold considerably aged by these two great blows. He is deafer and his memory is quite unpredictable. Unless very carefully and gently dealt with, he gets very upset. As you know, he was devoted to Karl Weber personally and they had grown much closer in the last year, so his death was a great personal sorrow, as well as being a worry in terms of the Jungfrau Lodge and all his belongings there. Of course we shall have to go to Murren for the K Jubilee, but Murren gets less and less attractive to him and I hope we shall be thinking in other alpine terms. The collapse of the A-K is also a tremendous blow to him. Of all his creations, I think he cherished it the most. Philippa may remember that when he retired from Chairmanship of the A-K Committee I said I gave the A-K five years to disintegrate. It has taken just that. I hope the Kandahar will not let the whole Jubilee fizzle out in the end. The Swiss seem more interested in Arnold's personal jubilee as an Editor. Perhaps Philippa could have a word with Peter Seligman, and Clarke and Elisabeth with Richard Hennings." Peter Seligman was Chairman of the Kandahar, and Peter Clarke was a Kandahar committee member who was also Secretary of The Times.

Richard Hennings was talking of retiring in 1974 and Lunn wrote to support the appointment of Elisabeth Hussey as Editor of Ski Survey. Joan Raynsford, the current Chairman, endorsed his recommendation, which was confirmed by the SCGB Council in February. Lunn sent a long "Memorandum on the Future of British Ski Racing" to be circulated to the SCGB Council and the Kandahar.

In February, Lunn went to a Dinner at St Catherine's College, Oxford to speak. He was in fine form, combining poetry with anecdotes. On 5 March, Shelby Cullom Davis, the US Ambassador to Switzerland, wrote congratulating him on a speech he had made in Bern. Bill Buckley had also been there. But by the end of March, Lunn was suffering considerable back pain. In April, he attended a Luncheon Party given by the Spanish Ambassador. In May, he resigned from the Kandahar Committee. The Club was by then planning to celebrate its 50th Anniversary.

Right up to May, he was busy writing to his friends. Courchevel was celebrating 25 years as a ski resort and the French Tourist Office sent him an invitation, saying his intuition had proved right. He said he could not remember ever going there, but it had probably been after Peter Lindsay had taken him to see Meribel in 1949.

By the end of May he was in hospital in London. A few days before he died he asked Phyllis to bring his typewriter to his hospital bed, so that he could continue to work more easily. Sigge Bergman, General Secretary of the FIS, received a letter from him on 27 May, ending with "I do hope we shall meet again soon." But Lunn was failing. A lifetime of neglecting his health, the effects of his fall in 1909 and cancer had all taken their toll. On 2 June 1974, aged 86, the end came.

Tributes were paid from all over the World. Lady Lunn collected quotes to publish from his friends and was particularly pleased when Marc Hodler, whom Lunn had often chided for not replying to correspondence, wrote back immediately in reply to her request. Tom Burns, responsible for publishing and selling many of his religious books, wrote: "He…had lived with a pentecostal flame within him ever since his conversion".

A Memorial Mass was held at Westminster Cathedral. The Cardinal Archbishop of Westminster attended and the Cathedral was packed with skiers, mountaineers, catholics and other friends.

Rosemary Tennant expressed the feeling of loss felt by many of his friends: "For those of us who worked with him in Hobart Place and Eaton Square, it will be the curious feeling of expectation, tempered with a faintly nervous anticipation, when we heard the familiar and unmistakable tread on the stairs, that we remember best and the enormous pleasure when we saw his head come round the door. It was as though the Club became more alive."

Lunn had left an unfinished book, which Lady Lunn finally published in 1977 with the help of James Hutchings. Called "The Enchanted Lakes", it covered Thun and Brienz.

A Memorial Fund was set up by the SCGB as so many people wanted to contribute. For many years an Annual Lecture was given in his memory. They were given by the Earl of Limerick, son of his old friend E.C. Pery,

George Cooper, Walter Amstutz, Marc Hodler and many other distinguished skiers.

Arnold Lunn's long and active life was filled with writing, travel and debate. The dominant themes were religion and skiing. When asked in 1974 whether he considered skiing to be the most important part of his life, he replied that religion was, and among the more than sixty books that he wrote many traced his conversion to Catholicism. But his incisive thought and tireless energy had also contributed to a revolution in winter sport. When we watch racers hurtling down steep mountainsides or weaving through slalom gates, we have him to thank for the most exciting spectacles in ski-racing!

Made in the USA
Charleston, SC
09 March 2015